David B. Ford

History of Hanover Academy

David B. Ford

History of Hanover Academy

ISBN/EAN: 9783337385958

Printed in Europe, USA, Canada, Australia, Japan

Cover: Foto ©ninafisch / pixelio.de

More available books at **www.hansebooks.com**

HISTORY

OF

HANOVER ACADEMY

BY

REV. D. B. FORD

Author of " New England's Struggles for Religious Liberty," etc.

BOSTON
H. M. HIGHT, PRINTER
319 Washington Street
1899

Price, fifty cents; sixty cents by mail

With great pleasure
do I dedicate this volume
to my friend

Eliza Smith (Salmond) Sylvester

by whose munificence
I am enabled to publish this work
at a price which is less than cost

PREFACE.

Hanover Academy, as compared with many of our higher seminaries and colleges, presents some advantages to the writer of its biography. In the first place, while much of its history may have been lost, yet its record has not in general been so darkened by the obscurity of a far distant past as to furnish any insuperable difficulty to its historian. Its existence does not antedate the century in which we live, and a venerable neighbor friend of mine, a stockholder in our Academic property, was born (1805) before Hanover Academy was built or thought of. Then, again, the Academy has had comparatively but a limited number of pupils. If it had numbered yearly its four or five hundred students, as Phillips Andover Academy now does, any minute history of it would be huge and unwieldly, and any condensed account of it would be meagre and uninteresting. Hanover Academy has lived long enough and has had numbers enough, both of teachers and scholars, to furnish an interesting variety of historic description. I have sought, so far as I was able, to make an interesting work, but never at the expense of decency or of truth. I have endeavored to write history, and even Don Quixote, of whom some remarkable vagaries are related, says that "History is a kind of sacred writing, because truth is essential to it, and where truth is, there God himself is;" but he goes on to say that "there are men who compose books and toss them out into the world like fritters." Again he says: "Let every man take care how he talks, or how he writes of other men, and not set down at random, higgedly-piggedly, whatever comes into his noddle." I think the following pages will give evidence that I have sought after facts, and that, as a result, the reader will have before him, in general, a veritable history of Hanover Academy. For the merits of this work, whatever they may be, I am indebted to a very large number of correspondents and friends, to all of whom I return my hearty thanks. Of those who have been especially helpful to me in certain ways, I may mention the names of Sara T. Chaddock of Portland, Me., Mrs. Abby L. Tyler of Boston, Mrs. Annie Richards Prime of Yonkers, N. Y., Hon. Charles A. Reed of Taunton, Mr. George Conant of Pasadena, Cal., William P. Duncan of Boston, Mrs. Royal Cheney of Worcester, Mrs. Luther Briggs, of Neponset, Dr. Henry L. Sweeny of Kingston, N. H., and L. Vernon Briggs of this place. Mr. Briggs has kindly loaned me many papers relating to our Academy students, which he doubtless will deposit in some of our public institutions. The many full and interesting letters relating to teachers and scholars which I have received but which could not be copied in full, I shall probably place in the archives of the New England Historic, Genealogical Society, 18 Somerset street, Boston.

PREFACE. 7

Some of our Academy pupils, I fear, will be disappointed in not finding their names recorded in this work. I can only say that no one would have been more glad than myself to have given the names and biographical sketches of ALL the Academy students, but the doing of this, owing to the absence of catalogues and lists, were an utter impossibility. The difficult matter of ascertaining, giving, withholding and omitting names has been my most serious trouble, as perchance the reader will discern before reaching the close of the book.

A word in regard to the portraits of the teachers.* Several of them have been recently taken, and I fear some of our older scholars will fail to recognize in them the teachers of their youth. The truth is, we all greatly change by advancing years, and had we not seen our faces in a mirror since we were young, we should, as strangers, have to be introduced to ourselves.

And now it only remains for me to say to my readers good-bye and farewell. This will doubtless be my *finis* effort in historic writing, and it is not without feeling that I send this, probably my last, work to the press. If my friends shall receive this work kindly I shall be thankful to have left with them this Souvenir (imperfect though it be) of a greatly cherished past.

DAVID B. FORD.

Hanover, Mass., Nov. 10, 1898.

*All the portraits in this work, with one exception, are from the Suffolk Engraving Company of Boston.

PART I.
HANOVER ACADEMY, 1808-18.
Its First Building and Teacher.

It is a matter of deep regret that, owing to the absence of records and the passing away of men, much of the history of Hanover Academy must forever remain unwritten and unknown. The fathers, and the mothers, too, where are they? and to whom or to what can we go for full information in regard to its early teachers? Some of them taught but for a brief period, and we scarcely know more than their names, and the probable time of their teaching. To this statement there is, however, one noted exception.

Of the REV. CALVIN CHADDOCK we have considerable information. Not only was he the founder and first teacher of the Academy, not only was his term of service a comparatively long one, from 1808 to 1818, but he was at the same time the pastor of a church, and he was, moreover, noted in an eminent degree, both as a teacher and preacher. His fame as an elocutionist has survived to the present hour. Scarcely could his hearers believe that any one else could read the Scriptures and Watts' Psalms and Hymns with such thrilling power and pathos as he. One can easily imagine how he, as a high-toned Calvinist, would sound out such lines as these:

>"Life, death and hell, and worlds unknown
> Hang on his firm decree;
> He sits on no precarious throne,
> Nor borrows leave to be."

Some one said of George Whitefield that he could pronounce the word " Mesopotamia " so as to make his hearers weep or tremble. Mr. Chaddock had similar elocutionary power, and few are the men who ever had his ability to stir the deep emotions of the human heart.

From a letter recently received from his daughter, Sara Thatcher Chaddock, now living in Portland, Me., from Chapman's Sketches of the Alumni of Dartmouth College, and from other sources, I learn that Mr. Chaddock (son of Capt. Joseph Chaddock who married Sara Bruce, and who died and was buried in Hanover, 1812, aged 88.) was born in Brookfield, Mass., in 1765, graduated at Dartmouth in 1791, received the honorary degree of A. M. from Brown University in 1801, studied divinity with the Rev. Dr. Nathaniel Emmons of Franklin, was ordained over the third Congregational church in Rochester, Mass., Oct. 10, 1793, in which place he also founded and taught an academy, was installed pastor at Hanover, July 23, 1806, was a representative to General Court in 1811, and was dismissed from his pastorate Ju'y 23, 1818. He was also a representative from Rochester in 1806.

Mr. Chaddock was a man of active and versatile powers, and, while a resident in Hanover, he was not only a preacher and teacher but, to some extent, a business man. In the Rev. Cyrus W. Allen's manuscript Historic Records, we read that he " entered somewhat into the business of weaving, taking materials in from places twenty or thirty miles distant and less, and letting out the work to others whom he employed to do it, a business which, if not so successful and profitable as hoped for, showed at least the peculiarities and capabilities of the man."

Owing, perhaps, to limited means and a large family,

he sought to better his circumstances by going where ministers were more needed. He first went to Marietta, O., suffering much through the exposures of a long and hard journey, from which he never recovered. Afterwards he was invited to Charleston, W. Va., where he was settled, and where on June 8, 1823, he died of consumption, and was buried by the side of two of his daughters. As stated in Rev. Mr. Barry's "History of Hanover," three of his daughters were married in that place. Some time after his death, the widow and a son, John, who was never married, and who was lost in a vessel sailing from San Francisco to Oregon, and the youngest daughter, Sara, returned to New England.

While in Virginia he was, of course, brought into contact with slavery. The following incident relating thereto is worthy of record. A slave who was spading his garden, having sought in vain permission of his master to buy himself, besought Mr. C. to intercede for him, which he did so effectually as to gain the master's consent. Shadrac, the slave, in about two years, by selling eggs, working nights and doing all sorts of labor, won his freedom, and then went to Ohio, where he bought an acre of ground, built a little hut, and in a few years bought his wife and children, and, to quote the language of the letter, "the poor fellow said that he owed it all to my father."

Mrs. Chaddock, whose maiden name was Melatiah Nye, and who was married to Mr. C. in 1792, was the daughter of Ebenezer Nye, of Oakham, Mass. He was captain of a company at the battle of Bunker Hill, and when a neighbor of his was shot down by his side on a retreat, he took the man on his back, carrying him thus till he was obliged to lay him down, and then took the buckles out of his shoes and carried them home as a memento to the poor soldier's wife. Mrs. Chaddock retained her church membership in Hanover until 1829, when she was dismissed to a church in New Bedford, in which place her son, Ebenezer Nye Chaddock, was living, and where she herself died, and was placed in a tomb with a sister, Mrs. Eli Haskell.

Mr. Barry gives the names of eight of their children, as if this were the full number. In Mr. L. Vernon Briggs' "Church and Cemetery Records" it is stated, probably on the authority of Rev. Samuel E. Evans, that there were twelve children as the result of their marriage. Miss Chaddock's letter substantiates the smaller number.

In the town library and in my own possession is a book entitled, "True Christianity, or the Whole Economy of God Towards Man, and the Whole Duty of Man Towards God, by Rev. John Arndt, translated into English and printed in London in 1712. First American edition revised and corrected by Rev. Calvin Chaddock of Hanover, Mass., 1809," with a preface by the editor.

Much that is interesting in regard to Mr. Chaddock both as a teacher and preacher, may be found in Mr. Barry's "History of Hanover," which we need not here repeat. I think it well, however, to print the following letter which was written the year our present Academy Building was dedicated, by "one of the earlier members of the Academy."

NEW CASTLE, N. H., Feb. 27, 1852.

MR. M. PARRIS McLAUTHLIN,—

Dear Sir : It would afford me much pleasure to attend the dedicatory services at the opening of your new Academy, agreeably to your polite invitation. But as this may not be, I will endeavor at your suggestion, to sketch a few reminiscences relative to its early history.

Though not of the first, yet I was among the earlier members of the Academy, having entered it on the 9th of June, 1812, about forty years ago.

The building, which was owned by subscribers and proprietors, was located near the centre of the town, a little west of the ancient parish church [where, according to our local historian, Mr. John Tower, " C. L. Tower's house now stands"]. It was tasteful, and even quite elegant, two stories high, of fair proportions, its walls neatly painted, furnished with Venetian blinds, and crowned with a cupola and bell. Within, at the end opposite the entrance, sat the Preceptor in an elevated desk, and on his right hand, in the extreme distance, was seated the Preceptress, with a group of young ladies, her pupils, before her. A respectable number of pupils, of both sexes, were in attendance from towns both of Plymouth and Norfolk counties.

Besides the common English branches, instruction was given in the Latin and Greek languages, in the higher mathematics, navigation, surveying, etc., and in the female department considerable attention was given to embroidery and painting in water colors.

These exercises were diversified by weekly declamations of a Wednesday afternoon, in the hall above, in the presence of the Preceptor, Preceptress, the pupils and visitors, who mingled in the group. The young ladies, with those of the other sex, took part in these exercises.

At the close of the term there was no public examination, but frequently an exhibition, as it was called. On those occasions, besides the declamation of individuals, there was usually a kind of theatrical performance, sometimes the acting of a drama. The attendance of spectators was large and from various towns.*

*Mrs. Abby L. (Hitchcock) Tyler of Boston writes me that her mother, while residing in her youth at North Pembroke, attended Mr. Chaddock's school, and that she and other schoolmates gave the play, " She Stoops to Conquer," herself being the Mrs. Hardcastle of the occasion.

From the same authority I learn that Mr. Chaddock's Latin class were required to address him in Latin, *e. g.*, when one wished to leave he would have to say, "*Licetne mihi, exire, O domine?*"

The young lady pupil above referred to, Miss Abigail L. Hall, in after years became the mother of one of our Academy teachers, Mr. Charles Hitchcock.

Of the former members of the Academy, my youthful associates, many have been useful citizens, and several somewhat distinguished in their professions.

I may thus mention Noah Torrey, Esq., long a highly respectable magistrate in Norfolk county; Rev. Reuben Torrey, a graduate at Providence of the class of 1816, and for many years a worthy pastor of a church in Connecticut; Dr. S. T. Angier, a graduate of the same University of the class of 1818; also my room-mate, Rev. Ira H. T. Blanchard, a graduate at Cambridge of the class of 1817, for some time a tutor in that University, and afterwards pastor of a church in Harvard.

"Of the honorable women, not a few," I may specially notice Mrs. Almira Little Torrey, whose amiable disposition, high intelligence, and devoted piety have embalmed her memory in the hearts of a numerous circle of friends, and who, by means of her interesting and published memoirs, "being dead, yet speaketh."

The venerable founder of Hanover Academy will not be forgotten either by those "who sat at his feet" as pupils, or were his hearers as a preacher of the Gospel.

His skill in sustaining the government and discipline of the school was admirable. To the minds of the youth in his charge he imparted the ardor of his own spirit in the pursuit of secular and sacred learning. With a mind richly gifted by the Father of Spirits, he possessed a native, simple, and truly genuine eloquence. His bosom, a fountain of the tenderest sympathies spontaneously gushing forth, moved him often and copiously to "weep with them that weep." To the afflicted—to the mourner in Zion—his words of consolation were the breathings of angelic sweetness; while the truth of God, heard from his lips in tones of deepest solemnity, thrilled the hearts of assembled multitudes. "Of like passions with others"—by no means faultless—yea, even specially "compassed with infirmity," yet in conflict with his spiritual foes "he was more than conqueror."

The peaceful close of his useful life was passed on the sunny plains of West Virginia. While passing up the beautiful Ohio, of a pleasant summer's morning, many years since, I was providentially thrown in company with some of those who enjoyed his last ministrations; and thus from the lips of his personal friends I received the animating account of his final exit from earth, in the triumph of Christian faith.

Most respectfully,

LUCIUS ALDEN.

HISTORY OF HANOVER ACADEMY. 15

Mr. Alden, one of the many boys fitted for college under Mr. Chaddock's tuition, was born in East Bridgewater, June 18th, 1796, graduated at Brown University 1821, and at Andover Theological Seminary in 1825; Home Missionary, Dearborn Co., Ind., 1825-30 ; pastor, East Abington, 1830-43, East Bridgewater, 1843-44, Lancaster, 1845, Newcastle, N. H., 1845-73 ; died at Brockton, April 24, 1884.

Mr. Reuben Torrey, mentioned in the letter, was born in Weymouth, April 3, 1789, was pastor in Eastford, Ct., in 1820-41, and subsequently in other towns of the same State. He died in Providence, R. I., Sept. 22, 1870. Samuel Tubbs Angier, M. D., was from Pembroke. Rev. Mr. Blanchard in 1842 preached for several months in East Bridgewater, but failing health forbade him to settle there. He died in 1845 in South Weymouth, his native town.

Almira Little, who married Rev. Joseph Torrey, of South Hanson, was one of a distinguished family of sisters, of whom some account is given in the Centennial History (1888) of the first Baptist church of Marshfield. I have seen and read her interesting Memoir. One of her sisters married Col. John Collamore, Esq., well known in this vicinity years ago, as county commissioner, and a deacon of the Baptist church in Hanover.

Another of Mr. Chaddock's pupils, Miss Eliza Hall, sister of Abigail above named, taught school for a long time. She was assistant for many years to a blind person, a Miss Baker, in a private school in New Bedford. One winter she studied Latin in the district school of North Pembroke, having a Mr. Deane, a Harvard student, as a teacher. She died at the age of 85, and during the last four years of her life she read Cicero and Virgil and many works in French.

What would we not give for a Historical Catalogue of all the pupils taught by Mr. Chaddock in Hanover? But, alas, we have not even a list of their names.

Probably it is not now generally known that Mr. Chaddock was at one time engaged in a very unpleasant law suit. The case of "Chaddock *versus* Briggs," was tried at Taunton in the July term of 1816, before the Supreme Judicial Court. It seems that Mr. Alden Briggs, Jr., of Pembroke, had more than once asserted in public that Mr. Chaddock (we omit the scurrilous terms employed) had been on a drunken frolic, that on one occasion while working in the meadow he was so drunk that he could not get home. Mr. C. sued him for slander, placing the damage at $2000, and procured Aaron Hobart, Esq., for his lawyer. In the complaint the plaintiff avers that he was always of good reputation and character for temperance and sobriety, and is and ever has been free from the odious and criminal offence of drunkenness, that he was in danger of being deprived of his ministerial office and losing the profits accruing to him from the same, and likewise that he has undergone great distress in body and mind, and has been greatly injured and prejudiced in his good name and in his religious character and usefulness. A verdict favorable to the plaintiff was rendered by the jury. Mr. Briggs' counsel, Benjamin Whitman, Esq., moved an arrest of judgment. He contended that the words spoken were not actionable, *per se*, especially when spoken of a Congregational minister, who cannot be said to have any tenure of office. Besides, the words did not indicate a habit but only a single act of frailty not inconsistent with the general character, and virtuous habits of a minister. Judge Isaac Parker maintained on the contrary that the office of a minister required a pure moral character, that even when not in the discharge of his ministerial functions he is to be under the control and obligations of the religion he professes to teach, and that a charge of this kind would certainly expose a minister to dismission from his people. He says that "by the verdict of the jury it is established that the defendant spoke the words alleged in reference to the plaintiff, and that they were falsely and maliciously spoken, and it is understood that an attempt which was made at the trial to justify the publishing by proving the truth of the words wholly failed." He further says that " the verdict in this case has established the malice ; and, indeed, from the opprobrious terms used in promulgating the fact, as well as the repetition of it in a form of words equally offensive, there was no room to suppose the defendant innocent of an evil intent in speaking them. Upon these grounds we are satisfied that the delaration is sufficient, and the motion in arrest of judgment must be overruled." Thankful may we be for such a triumphant defence of the accused! Yet it is perhaps but fair to say that some even now believe, on what they regard as adequate testimony, that there was some truth in the above charge. For a report of this trial, see 13 Mass. p. 248 of the Social Law Library in the Court House, Boston.

I have met with some aged persons who were enthusiastic in their admiration for Mr. Chaddock as a preacher. Surely as a teacher, also, he deserves the high admiration and regard of all our people.

" The town," says Mr. Barry, " has reason to rememher him with gratitude for his patient and earnest efforts for the improvement of the young." Especially may we be thankful that as a pioneer he started an influence in favor of higher education which has spread far and wide, and which has already lasted nearly a hundred years. Had it not been for him, Hanover might have had a far different educational history.

I am sorry to learn that no likeness of Mr. Chaddock is now in existence—"the large-sized painting" spoken of in Mr. Barry's history having gone to utter decay and ruin. He is described as being rather short and thickset, but as having a very fine figure. The best thing I can do to represent, perchance, something of his looks is to insert here his youngest daughter's picture, taken, as she says, when "in my prime." She writes that she was christened Sally Thatcher Chaddock, but, as she thinks Sara the prettier name, she is now so called by her friends. She says that she has no talent for writing ?), and that all the talent she has is dramatic, which she inherited from her father. Her friends speak of her as being an excellent reader.

MISS CHADDOCK.

I sometimes fancy that the existence and influence of Hanover Academy, as conducted by Mr. Chaddock and his successors, had something to do with the holding of an all-day educational meeting, September, 1838, in the Episcopal Church at our "Four Corners," which was attended by no less dignitaries than Daniel Webster and John Quincy Adams, and also the Hon. Horace Mann, if I mistake not. Mr. Webster, who was on that occasion evidently suffering from asthma or hay fever, did not show much animation in his speaking, especially as contrasted with Mr. Adams, who, in mind and body was all activity. The following extract from Mr. Adams' speech, which we take from a manuscript copy, may be of some interest to our readers :

"There was one usage in the ancient republic of Sparta which now occurred to him and which filled his mind with this pleasing idea, namely, that these endeavors of ours for the fit education of all our children, would be the means of raising up a generation around us which would be superior to ourselves. The usage was this : The inhabitants of the city on a certain day collected together and marched in procession, dividing themselves into three companies, the old, the middle-aged, and the young. When assembled for the sports and exercises, a dramatic scene was introduced, and the three parties each had a speaker, and Plutarch gives the form of phraseology used in the several addresses on the occasion. The old men speak first, and addressing those beneath them in age, say :

' We have been in days of old,
Wise, generous, brave and bold.'

Then come the middle-aged, and casting a triumphant look at their seniors, say to them :

'That which in days of yore ye were,
We at the present moment are.'

Lastly march forth the children, and looking bravely on both companies who had spoken, they shout forth thus :

"Hereafter, at our country's call,
We promise to excel you all.'"

In connection with a reference to the influence of Mr. Chaddock, it should be stated that his descendants have ever manifested a deep interest in the welfare of the Academy. His daughter, Roxana, wife of Hon. Albert Smith, was a generous donor to its funds; and his granddaughter, Mrs. Annie L. (Smith) Bigelow, late deceased, often remembered the needs of the students. Indeed, nearly all the scholarships which have been granted to the students have come as gifts either from Mrs. Bigelow or from Mrs. Eliza Salmond.

After Mr. Chaddock's departure the school rapidly declined. It is thought that Rev. Mr. Chapin, the successor of Mr. Chaddock, taught there for a brief period, and that it was used at times for a Sunday school ; and thus it was suffered to remain until about the year 1822, when it was sold and moved to the Four Corners. In early times it was utilized by Mr. Ephraim Stetson for the storage and sale of strong waters,* and on these "Stetson Shoals," as the place was called, many a poor ship carpenter met with serious if not fatal shipwreck. It was subsequently lengthened out on its eastern end, (the cut below shows about the whole length of the original building. The piazza is, of course, a modern addition,) and in later years was occupied as a store and shoe manufactory by Mr. Stephen Josselyn, but is now used as a drug store by Mr. William Snow Curtis. The

*It is reported for a truth that these waters were, at least in very cold weather, so weak that they were unable to run.

bell, with its sharp, ringing sound, was probably transferred to the new Academy building, of which we shall next speak.

THE FIRST ACADEMY BUILDING.

PART II.

HANOVER ACADEMY, 1828-51.

Its Second Building and its Teachers.

This second building was erected in 1828, ten years after Mr. Chaddock's leaving Hanover, and it stood on the east side of Broadway Street, about midway between the dwelling of J. Williams Beal and the Odd Fellows' Hall, nearly at the foot of the present Academy Avenue. It consisted of two stories, and in outward appearance it resembled, as I should suppose, the old one, save that it was somewhat larger.

It would be interesting to know who started this enterprise, and what were the inducements for so doing. It is thought by some that Rev. Mr. Wolcott, who perhaps at that time was teaching a private school near by, greatly favored and helped on the movement, and that possibly his feelings were somewhat hurt that he was not earlier invited to become its teacher. In a letter dated Nov. 3d, 1858, written by Charles A. Reed, the then Preceptor of the Academy, to Mr. Wolcott, inviting him to a reunion of the Alumni on Nov. 26th, he says: "Be assured that we would be exceedingly gratified to meet you at this reunion, and would welcome you to the hospitalities of Hanover, as one of the founders of our institution." All the shareholders of this property, thirty-nine in number, and embracing some of the most substantial men of the time, have passed away, and in these matters of inquiry we are left to our own conjectures.

These proprietors belonged principally to the three towns of Hanover, Scituate and Pembroke, and since the "Four Corners" serves as a central position for these towns, the building, doubtless for this reason mainly, was located here. It was built, according to Mr. Barry's History, in shares of $25 each, at an expense of about $1,200; the Trustees were incorporated in 1829; and the names of the original proprietors were Alexander Wood, Esq., Capt. Haviland Torrey, Joseph Eells, Ephraim Stetson, Dr. Ezekiel Cushing, Rev. Calvin Wolcott, Sarah Gardner (Wolcott?), Robert Eells, Asaph Magoun, Horace Collamore, Esq., Gen. A. W. Oldham, Capt. Tilden Crooker, Benjamin C. Pratt, Ethan A. Stetson, Capt. William Josselyn, Eli Stetson, Joseph S. Bates, Horatio Cushing, Esq., Isaac Magoun, Col. John B. Barstow, Capt. Thomas Waterman, Capt. Nathaniel Barstow, John C. Stockbridge, George Bailey, Dr. Joseph Studley, Justus Whiting, Thomas Damon, Benjamin Mann, Esq., Lemuel Dwelley, (Col.) Samuel Tolman, Jr., Elias W. Pratt, Luther Howland (of Hanson), James Waterman, Samuel Waterman, Samuel Stetson, Elias Magoun, John Barstow, Esq., Albert Clapp, and John Wilder.

Perhaps if the former building had been for sale at this time, it might have been purchased for the new school. This new building was used continuously for a school some twenty-three years. The shareholders were incorporated February 18th, 1828, and Alexander Wood, Horatio Cushing, John B. Barstow, Col. Samuel Tolman, Jr., and Horace Collamore, were chosen as a Board of Trustees.

ITS TEACHERS.

We are sorry that we cannot now tell more about its

earlier teachers. Several of them, as it would seem, taught but for a short time.*

The first teacher, ZEPHANIAH AMES BATES (1828), (not Bass, as in Barry's History), was the son of Joshua and Bethiah (Ames) Bates, and was born in Hanover, 1803, graduated from Harvard College, 1824, and after leaving here went South as a teacher, and died there in 1842. He was never married. Near relatives of his are still living in Bridgewater, with one of whom, Sarah T. Bates, a niece, I have had some correspondence.

MR. HORACE HALL ROLFE (1829), son of Rev. William and Judith (Hazletine) Rolfe, was born at Groton, July 24, 1800, graduated at Dartmouth College, 1824, and died in Charleston, S. C., February 24, 1831. In March, 1828, he married Mary Marcy, of Plymouth (where he had taught for a time), and while in Hanover they lived in the Seth Barker (Horatio Bigelow) house, near North River Bridge—the same house in which Mrs. Wade subsequently kept a private school.†

*The order of teachers and dates of their teaching, as given in Rev. Mr. Barry's History of Hanover, are approximately correct. I was in hopes to get some material for our Academy History from the collection of documents made by Mr. Barry, but I learn that there is nothing left which would be serviceable. I may state as a matter of interest to many, that one of his daughters, Caroline L. Barry, now Mrs. C. L. Morton (widow), of Longwood, Florida, was for a short time an Academy student. Another daughter, Eliza B. Barry, is living with her mother, Mrs. Louisa Barry, in Newtonville. I think there are also other daughters.

†Mrs. Charlotte S. (Brown) Wade, was the young widowed consort of Dr. Henry Wade, who practised in Hanover in 1829, and died in 1830. Her school bore the somewhat ambitious title of "Plymouth County Seminary," but, from what I have heard, she was well deserving to be at the head of such an institution. As she had the happy faculty of adapting herself to all ages, she was

Passing by the name of REV. CYRUS HOLMES (1830) of whom we shall speak later on, we come next to MR. ETHAN ALLEN (1830). I have in my possession a receipt from him, dated April 19th, 1830, for tuition of my eldest brother : " Six weeks, $1.50 ; for bell-ringing, wood, etc., $0.10 ; total $1.60. Received payment." Mr. Allen was born in Londonderry, Vt., Nov. 25, 1794, was graduated at Brown University in 1823, and after teaching in Millwood, Va., in Hanover, and in Rochester, N. Y., was ordained an Episcopal minister, and afterwards served as pastor in Otis, 1836—46, in Nantucket 1846—55, and in Guilford, Vt., where he died May 19, 1867.

The REV. CALVIN WOLCOTT (1831), appears next as the teacher for one year. He was for a long time a resident of this place, serving as rector of St. Andrew's

greatly beloved by all her scholars. Her system of teaching was peculiarly unique, original, and interesting, and it was a pleasure to be under her instruction. (Substance of a letter received from Mrs. Adeline Briggs.) Another of her pupils, mentioned below, says that " Mrs. Wade was a woman of high cultivation, belonging to one of the first families of Hingham, a lady of great executive ability, and one who, wherever she was placed, attracted the attention of all who saw her, yet seemingly unconscious of it herself." She was subsequently invited by the Society of Friends to open a school in New Bedford, which she conducted until her marriage to a Friend, Isaac Taber of that place. She would have served well as Preceptress of the Academy had such an arrangement been then in fashion. During her term of teaching (1830—4) the Academy was obliged to have several different male teachers. For a part of the time her school was quite large, and she had one of her graduate pupils, Miss Judith S. Cook, now living in Boston, for an assistant, to whom Mrs. Wade left the charge of the school, and who finally went to New Bedford to be her assistant there. Certainly this school should not be overlooked in summing up the educational influences which have left their stamp on the minds of this community.

Church, from 1818 to 1834. I have fortunately obtained many facts concerning his history from his granddaughter, Mrs. Annie Richards Prime, of Yonkers, N. Y., the daughter of Dr. Jacob and Elizabeth G.(Wolcott) Richards, of Braintree. His remote ancestor in this country was William Wolcott (or Walcott), of Salem, 1636. His grandfather was Jonathan Wolcott, who was born in Danvers and died in Windham, Ct., May 25, 1745. His father, Elijah Wolcott, lived and died in Williamsburg, Mass. Mr. Wolcott was born in Williamsburg, April 27, 1787, and died in New York City, January 21, 1861. In 1811 he was married to Sarah Gardner, of Danvers, who, according to Mr. Barry, was a collateral descendant of Gen. Putnam. He entered Phillips Andover Academy, Aug. 12, 1809, left the school in 1811, subsequently studied theology under the direction of Bishop Griswold, and then made his first settlement in Hanover. After leaving here he officiated in the churches in Otis and Blandford, in the western part of the State, became rector of Christ's Church in Quincy, and in Hopkinton, Vt., resigning the latter church about 1844.* Then for some years he served as general agent of the American Bible society in Massachusetts and Western Virginia. In 1850 he received a call from his old friend, Rev. Dr. Stephen H. Tyng, of St. George's Church, New York, to become assistant minister, which office he resigned about 1859, on account of ill-health, but continued to live in the city till his death. His remains were taken to Quincy and placed in the Richards' family vault, in the old cemetery. A long time resident in Hanover when in the

---

*See History of St. Andrew's Church by Rev. Samuel Cutler, 1848.

prime of life, he is even now well remembered in this place, and is highly esteemed by many who were his hearers or his pupils. Of Mr. Wolcott's sons, two, Samuel G. and Asa G., became distinguished physicians, and one, George T., taught for a brief space in our Academy.

For a winter or more Mr. Wolcott taught school on "Church Plain," in Scituate (afterward South Scituate, and now Norwell), and he also had a private school in the attic of his own house, corner of Broadway and Oakland Avenue. He was, as I should judge, a very nervous man, and was at times very severe in his punishments, the which, if attempted now in our schools, would not be long endured. Facing the cold north-west wind in winter as he walked over "Church Hill" in the morning, was, no doubt, trying to his feelings, and for this reason, or some other, he would occasionally omit morning prayer, and when this happened we knew what to expect. Woe to that scholar whose eye he, while engaged as the first thing in ruling the writing books, would detect looking off from his book. And yet he was generally so pleasant and "clever" in the school-room, and withal so good a teacher, that his scholars, almost without exception, liked him and loved him. In the attic library of my present residence, I presume there may be found two or three small New Testaments of a faded red binding, which are inscribed with his name, and which he gave to us boys as a reward "for diligence and good behavior." While we can justly say that he was successful as a teacher, it can also be truly said that his church enjoyed a good degree of prosperity under his long pastorate.

JOHN P. WASHBURN (1832), was born in Ware, April

8, 1855, and died in Barnstable, April 14, 1886. After leaving Hanover he taught for a while at Scituate Harbor. While teaching in these places he was, according to report, pursuing the study of medicine. He subsequently taught in Bridgewater, Sandwich, and several other towns, especially on the Cape. In Sandwich, in 1835, he married for his first wife Patience W. Crocker, who died September 14, 1875, aged nearly 69 years. They had four children, two of whom died in infancy, and two daughters are now living. In May 4, 1879, he married Martha N. Hinckley, of Barnstable, who still survives. In his later years he was engaged in the insurance business in Barnstable.

DR. IRA WARREN (1833), was born in Canada, 1805, studied for a time in Brown University, taught school at Queen Anne's Corner, in Hingham, became preceptor for about a year in Hanover Academy, married in 1834 a village maiden, Miss Ruth Stockbridge Turner, subsequently taught in the Academy at Edgartown, and then went to Boston, where he studied medicine, and where he practised as a physician till his death in 1864. His remains are interred in our Hanover cemetery. While in Boston he edited for a time "The Christian Witness" (Episcopalian), and wrote two books, "Puseyism, its Causes and Cure," and "The Household Physician," a large volume which has had an immense sale. I may say that Mr. Warren in his early manhood resided for some years at Hanover Corners, where I first became acquainted with him. He then seemed to me to be rather a man of thought than of action. His subsequent life and writings prove that on the first point at least I was not mistaken. One of our Alumni, a man of discernment and sound judgment, who resided for a time in his family (George F. Stetson, of Hanson), in a letter to me, characterizes him as "a clear and careful thinker, a cultured, independent, and able writer, an instructive conversationalist, and altogether a refined, sympathetic and charming friend and gentleman." I am sorry that I cannot obtain his portrait for this work, but it can be found in the medical treatise above mentioned.

THOMAS FULLER WHITE.

THOMAS FULLER WHITE (1834—37) son of Abiel and Joanna (Fuller) White, was born in Halifax, July 29, 1810, died in Cumberland, Md., December 26, 1864. He was of Pilgrim descent, his maternal ancestor being Deacon and Doctor Samuel Fuller, who came over in the Mayflower. Educated at Northampton, he early betrayed an aptitude and fondness for teaching, and began this calling in several towns of Plymouth County, one of his schools being in North Pembroke. His success in teaching led to his becoming principal of Hanover Academy in 1834. He appears to have been eminently skilful both in governing easily and in successful teaching, qualities as diverse in their nature as are the wisdom of the serpent and the harmlessness of the dove. His system of instruction, it is thought, would not suffer in comparison with any of the modern methods of education. His quarterly examinations and exhibitions seem to have been red-letter occasions for the Academy. He is described as being a gentleman of fine personal appearance, of cultivated and graceful manners, and, indeed, as a person who apparently had no mean opinion of himself. Being also an accomplished reader and a fluent speaker, he was naturally often called upon to make addresses on public occasions. While teaching in Duxbury in 1832 he was appointed by Gov. Levi Lincoln as adjutant of 1st Regiment Infantry, 1st Brigade, 5th Division of the Massachusetts Militia, and was honorably discharged therefrom January, 1837. Resigning the Principalship of the Academy this same year, he accepted a professorship of Latin and Greek, at Charlotte Hall, Calvert County, Md., but removed the following year to Cumberland of the same State, to become the principal of the Alleghany County Academy. For the improvement of his health he afterwards engaged in civil engineering, and pursued that calling until his decease. In Cumberland he served one term as Mayor, but declined re-election. In 1861 he was appointed surveyor of Alleghany County. Though engrossed with business he was an earnest worker in the Temperance and other good causes, and was a devoted and efficient member of the Episcopal Church.

In November, 1841, he married Mrs. Mary Thistle Hilary, and has had a large family of daughters, several of whom died in infancy. Two became popular and successful teachers, and two are residing in Cumberland with their aged mother. I should have stated that Mr. White, though living in a slave State in war times, was unswerving in his devotion and loyalty to the Union.*

HERMAN BOURN(1836-37) son of Andrew and Lucinda (Barrows) Bourn, was born in Attleboro, Jan. 9, 1800, and was graduated from Brown University, class of 1825. The college catalogue latinizes his given name to *Hermannus*, and simply states that he was from Attleboro. Mr. Bourn is described as being a very sedate, quiet, dignified person, talented and scholarly. He was the author of a work on Botany which, for those days, was nicely gotten up and handsomely illustrated.

A few years since I was informed by a keeper of minerals and curios, in Boston, that he had in his possession a pen-written list of students in the male department of Hanover Academy, for the Second or Fall term, commencing Monday, August 7, and ending Saturday, October 28, 1837. Recently I visited the city store and purchased this interesting document—the first list of Academy boyswhich I have ever seen. This list, remarkable for its chirography, was evidently written by the teacher, Mr. Bourn, and is substantially correct, though some few names as here recorded *literatim*, are not fully and accurately written :

Stephen N. Gifford, George Studley, Luther Briggs,

---

*For many of the facts in Mr. White's history I am indebted to his niece, Miss H. E. Bruce, and to Mr. and Mrs Luther Briggs, all of Neponset.

Francis Collamore, Augustus Collamore, Theodore Collamore, Robert Barstow, Joseph B. Barstow, Joseph Dwelley, Henry Bates, William Josselyne, James Tolman, Tobias O. Gardner, John A. Smith, James R. Smith, Joseph B. Sylvester, Belcher Magoon, Luther Studley, John D. Twiggs, George W. Eels, Andrew I. Sprague, *Sarah E. Barstow*, *Priscilla B. Smith*, Austin Dyer, Robert Dwelly, Jonathan Oldham, Thomas H. Soule, Henry C. Wainwright, John E. Barstow, Horace Stetson, Eleazer Josslyne, Asa C. Hammond, Charles I. Hilburn, Robert Salmon, Alden Briggs 3d, Benjamin Elliot.

Miss HANNAH W. JOHNSON (1837), was for two terms a contemporary teacher with Mr. Bourn at the Academy. In her second term, ending in September, she had 25 young lady students. Among the scholars of Miss Johnson, as also of Miss Fuller at a later period, I notice the names of Lydia K. and Elizabeth T. Barstow, of Providence, daughters of John Barstow, Esq., who many years afterward established a fund for the Hanover Academy. From the accounts given of Miss Johnson by her pupils, I should judge her to have been an excellent teacher. The closing words of the valedictory address, spoken by Miss Adeline Collamore, were without doubt sincerely and truthfully spoken. Addressing her associates in study she says:

" Let us express our gratitude to her who so long and faithfully instructed us. Accept our thanks, dear teacher, for your unwearied exertions in promoting useful knowledge among us, for your forbearance with our many faults, and for the schemes you have continually devised for our improvement and happiness while under your care. It is with unmeasured feelings of regret that we now bid you farewell, and while distance shall separate us from you, ever indulge the assurance that in the hearts of your pupils, your memory is cherished with gratitude and affection." And in one of several helpful letters recently received from her, now Mrs. Adeline (Collamore) Briggs of Neponset, she thus speaks: "Under Miss Johnson's excellent tuition in Hanover's classic halls, my school days ended. The memory of those days is to me an ever recurring delight and will always be held in grateful remembrance. As a teacher, she was most successful in winning the love and confidence of her pupils. Uniformly kind and courteous, of a sweet and lovable disposition, she won all hearts at once. The hardest task became a pleasure under her encouraging guidance." Another of her pupils, but evidently one of the youngest class, has a distinct recollection that she had "very red hair." She afterward taught in Salem, N. H., and then obtained a very desirable situation as private instructress in the family of a wealthy rice planter residing in Georgetown, S. C.

We herewith give a list of Miss Johnson's pupils, as preserved by one of the scholars, Julia Collamore, sister of the above named valedictorian—the first list of the Academy female students which has come to my knowledge.

Adeline Collamore, Julia Collamore, Sylvia B. Waterman, Elizabeth Dwelley, Jane Hersey, Lydia Church, Louisa Bowker, Huldah Stetson, Amelia Josselyn, Amelia Barstow, Elizabeth Barstow, Louisa Wood, Eliza Hobart, Louisa Farnham, Eliza Dyer, Cynthia Dyer, Sarah A. Bates, Jane R. Oldham, Lois C. Stetson, Helena M. T. Eells, Sarah Barstow, Harriet Barstow, Lydia W. Collamore, Celia Percival, Lydia K. Barstow, Elizabeth T. Barstow, Helen Smith, Louisa Clark, Sarah Hitchcock, Polly B. Talbot, Judith Hammond, Mary Stetson, Susan Turner (of Pembroke).

JOSIAH FULLER (1838-39) the son of Robert and Rhoda (French) Fuller, and grandson of Dr. Noah Fuller of Wrentham, Mass., and Westmoreland, N. H., was born in Westmoreland. After leaving Hanover he went to Honolulu, S. I., where he edited a paper and was superintendent of the Royal Schools during the reign of Kamehameha III, who was a fast friend of the missionaries. I am told that he there married Margaret Mills of Natick, Mass., who went to Honolulu to visit her sister, the wife of Rev. S. C. Damon, D. D., the Seaman's chaplain of that place. They had two sons, who are married and still live in Honolulu; also a daughter, Elizabeth, who died in California. He became interested in the California mines and finally moved to Oakland, Cal., where he died some ten years since.

Before coming to Hanover, Mr. Fuller taught the Union Bridge District School in Scituate, and boarded with a relative of mine, by which means I first became acquainted with him. By virtue of this aquaintance, I was induced to attend the Academy when it came under his supervision. Here was the turning point of my life. Had it not been for his boarding where he did, had it not been for this Academy and his coming here as a teacher, I probably should have remained on the "Bald Hill Farm" all the rest of my days. How strange that one little thing will so affect our entire destiny! Not only so, but the mystery of life is such that, methinks, it takes ten thousand little things to place us where we are and to make us what we are. And so it has been with all our ancestors!

Mr. Fuller's sister Elizabeth kept a female school in the upper hall. In her third and last term she had 28 pupils. She subsequently married Calvin McQuestion, M. D., of Hamilton, Canada, who died some years since. Afterwards, she went to live with her niece, Mrs. Archibald McKeand (née Currier) of Chicago, and is now deceased.

A list of Miss Fuller's scholars is also given by Miss Collamore. Among them we find the following new names:

Angeline Peterson, Mercy Wright, Mary Cushing, Lydia Clark, Ann S. Dwelley, Caroline Hildreth, Harriet Hildreth, Elizabeth Torrance, Rachel A. Fuller, Lucy Josselyn, Elizabeth Stetson, Deborah Briggs, Nancy Percival, Mary Salmond, Elizabeth Eells, Abby Pratt, Elizabeth Pratt, Lucy Dyer, Sarah Dyer, Eliza Talbot, Frances Cushing, Mary J. Hilborn, Eliza Ellis, Lucy E. Boynton, Grace F. Barstow.

The outlines of REV. CYRUS HOLMES' life are given in Mr. Barry's Hanover History. He was born in Halifax, July 9, 1800, studied at Phillips Exeter Academy, graduated (according to Barry) at Dartmouth, 1828,[*] and at Andover Theological Seminary in 1831, taught in Woburn 1831-35 and Northampton, preached for a while until his health failed him, and then came to Hanover in 1840 and was Principal of the Academy for some eight years, until 1848, the year before his death. So highly was he esteemed by his fellow-citizens that

---

[*] I only find that Dartmouth College conferred upon him the honorary degree of A. M. in 1835. His name does not appear on the list of graduates.

without his seeking, he was elected as Representative to our Legislature for 1848-9. I had just made a beginning in Latin under Mr. Fuller, but it was under Mr. Holmes' tuition that I mainly received my fitting for college.

Mr. Holmes was a unique personality. Coming into the school room the first morning, and in marked contrast with his immediate predecessor, he seemed to us

REV. CYRUS HOLMES.

quite farmer-like in look and dress and slightly unkempt in appearance, and we were at first somewhat abashed. But we soon found out that he was a man of keen intellectual powers, of scholarly attainments, and a very superior teacher who had a most happy and effective use of the tongue. He had but little need of high-priced, complicated philosophical apparatus for instructive teaching. With his pencil or a chip or a piece of coal or something equally simple, he could illustrate much which admitted of illustration. A line from one of his pupils who subsequently became a teacher, Mr. Andrew T. Magoun, shows how interesting and deeply instructive was Mr. Holmes in his (ethical) teaching of one branch of English Grammar. "We used to parse out of Young's Night Thoughts.* Sometimes we would have quite an interesting discussion. Mr. Holmes liked to have each one express his views freely. I recollect on one occasion he said he would as soon think of eating a quarter of beef at a meal as of reading Young's Night Thoughts without pondering the subject under consideration."

Mr. Holmes also had but little use for the rattan. With his tongue he could shame and subdue the most refractory and grind out a tear from the most stubborn and obdurate, and he would seldom quit a subject of discipline until he had accomplished his purpose. On one occasion, when a girl named Ruth———had been acting naughtily, he proposed to preach a short sermon to the school, and said he would take his text from the book of Ruth: BE ASHAMED. I believe the text cannot be found there, but Ruth was most thoroughly ashamed. The two girls who in sport forged a letter purporting to be from a young man, inviting a certain academy girl with whom he had no acquaintance to

---

* Speaking of "parsing," reminds me of a little incident in my own experience in that line under Mr. Holmes. I was giving the "subject nominative" of a Greek verb, which, by an indistinct pronunciation might stand either for we or you (in Greek hemeis or humeis). Perhaps, as being a little uncertain, I pronounced the word somewhat indistinctly; whereupon I was asked: "What kind of *meis* (mice) Ford?" "He-meis," was my reply, which was correct.

take a beach ride—which letter was taken in earnest—will never forget the flood of tears which were shed before their teacher got done with them. Other anecdotes in regard to Mr. Holmes can be found in a commemorative poem on a later page.

Still, Mr. Holmes' spirit and manner were ever genial and gentle, and his pleasant and brilliant repartees and off-hand sayings were indescribable and can never be forgotten by those who heard them. It is almost needless to say that as a teacher and companion, he was to an unusual degree, beloved and respected by his pupils. I have enjoyed the instruction of Dr. Francis Wayland and of other distinguished teachers, but I never lost my regard and respect for Mr. Holmes.* With

---

*Well do I recollect the day when a lad, making my first visit to Providence, 1841, before there were any railroads in Plymouth county (the "Old Colony" being opened in 1846 and the "Hanover Branch" in 1868) I took a stage-coach to Taunton, and passing by the Academy building, beheld Mr. Holmes coming out of school that by his presence he might give me his kindly benediction. What that student lad, in after years accomplished, especially in the way of literary effort—all too meagerly and imperfectly—may be learned in part from the following sketch of his public life as given substantially in the Historical Catalogue of Brown University:

David Barnes Ford, A. B. 1845 (A. M. 1848, D. D. 1898) graduated Newton Theological Institution 1848; assistant instructor in Hebrew, Newton, 1848 and 1849; ordained Baptist, 1851; pastor, Canton, Mass., 1851-1854; for several years a supply in Marshfield, Mass. Author: Perthes' *Life of Chrysostom*, translated in conjunction with Alvah Hovey, 1854; *Studies on the Baptismal Question* with Review of J. W. Dale, 1879; *Centennial History of First Baptist Church, Marshfield*, 1888; *Commentary on Romans*, in conjunction with Prof. A. N. Arnold, 1889; *The Life-Work of Isaac Backus*, with Memorial Exercises at the dedication of the Backus Monument, 1893; *New England's Struggles for Religious Liberty*, 1896; *The Meetings of the Warren Association in the Old Colony*, 1896; Contributor to the Christian Review, Bibliotheca Sacra, and other periodicals.

the exception of Mr. Chaddock, his term of teaching here was longer than that of any other Principal of the Academy. Mr. Holmes died Aug. 16, 1849, and was buried in Pembroke Centre cemetery, where the remains of his wife, Sophia (Collamore) Holmes have since been placed by his side. The accompanying portrait of Mr. Holmes was taken from a somewhat faded daguerreotype, but I think it looks quite life-like. He was a person of medium height, of spare build, having bright, dark eyes and a thin face which was slightly sallowish in complexion, the result, perhaps, of long continued ill-health.

The same methodical and careful one who has given us the preceding lists, has also preserved the names of Mr. Holmes' pupils who attended the first two terms :

Samuel Tolman, David B. Ford, Augustus Collamore, Francis Collamore, Theodore Collamore, Robert Hersey, Robert Sylvester, Charles Torrey, Bailey H. Hitchcock, Robert S. Curtis, Joseph Barstow, Frederic O. Barstow, James Turner, Elisha Stetson, James R. Smith, Edmund Q. Sylvester, Edward Barstow, Robert Barstow, Joshua Fuller, Joshua J. Ellis, Charles Brooks, William Clark, Franklin E. Felton, Cyrus Morton, John B. Bates, Samuel House, Robert Salmond, Walter Clift.

Only two new names of female students are recorded: Priscilla Clark and Ann Eliza Josselyn.

I know of no list of students kept by Mr. Holmes during his many years of teaching. And about half the teachers who have taught since, even though they may have kept lists, have not left any behind them to my knowledge. It is a source of unfeigned regret to me that I cannot give all the names of our Academy stu-

dents, especially as I can think of very many whom I
would delight to mention.

After the preceding paragraph was in type I received
from Mr. Holmes' daughter, Sophia A., wife of Mr.
Emmons Hatch, of Winchester, a list of names taken
from an Album bed-quilt which was presented to Mr.
Holmes in 1848, the last year of his teaching, by his
students in the Academy. This list of names, though
amounting to some seventy in number, does not of
course give but a small part of all his Academy
scholars.

Elizabeth T. Waterman, Samuel G. Cutler, Albert B.
Howland, John B. Bates, Henry Clark, Mary Pratt,
Lucy S. Dyer, Betsey S. Magoun, Mary Collamore, Elizabeth C. Sturtevant, Chloe S. Perry, Jared Gardner,
Priscilla Eells, Helena M. Eells, Ruth M. Eells, Anna
L. Eells, Sarah A. Bates, Haviiand Barstow, Harriet R.
Blackman, Reuben Bates, Sarah H. Collamore, George
A. Collamore, Julia Collamore, Robert S. Curtis, Mary
A. Clark, Marcia Collamore, Sophia B. Clark, Huldah
B. Dwelley, George R. Dwelley, Charles Dyer, R. Cornelia Dyer, Nathan H. Dwelley, William P. Duncan,
Dorothy B. Dyer, Frederick Hatch, Henry Hersey,
Louisa E. Hatch, Lucinda Hatch, Marcia Josselyn,
George S. Josselyn, Eliza A. Josselyn, M. Josephine
Josselyn, Ann R. Haynes, Hulda S. Magoun, Nancy
W. Percival, Emmeline A. Pratt, Elias E. Pratt, Davis D.
Randall, B. F. Sylvester, Joseph C. Stockbridge, Sarah
M. Sturtevant, Sarah J. Sylvester, Alphonso F. Sturtevant, W. H. Stetson, Catherine A. Stetson, Mary Salmond, Hulda M. Stetson, I. B. Talbot, James Turner,
A. H. Talbot, E. S. Talbot, Edward F. Wood, William
B. Wood, Henry A. Wood, Lydia C. Waterman, Joseph

E. Wilder, Isaac Wilder, Thomas B. Waterman, William C. Oakman, Jr.

Mr. Holmes, as we have said, died Aug 16, 1849. We subjoin a Song by an unknown writer, "Respectfully Dedicated to the Memory of the late Rev. Cyrus Holmes," which was sung to the tune of "Long, Long Ago," at the Academy Exhibition, Oct. 12, 1849:

> " Kind was the heart which in sympathy beat:
> Now it is still—it is still.
> Sweet was the smile which we all loved to greet:
> But it has fled—it has fled.
> Past are those moments of social delight,
> Faded and fled are the scenes once so bright.
> Shrouded the brightness of morning in night:
> For he is gone—he is gone.
>
> Weep not for him when you stand by his grave.
> He has gone home—has gone home.
> Bright is his crown in the home of the saved.
> He has gone home—has gone home.
> Peaceful his rest in the home of the dead.
> Peaceful the shadows that fall on his bed,
> Weep not for him, for the spirit has fled
> Up to its home—to its home.
>
> Weep not for him when you muse on the past.
> He has gone home—has gone home.
> Joy that his sufferings are ended at last,
> And he's gone home—he's gone home.
> Let each memento of him who has gone—"

(The remaining lines of the stanza are wanting in the copy which I have quoted).

MR. CHARLES HITCHCOCK (1848-49) while pursuing the studies of the Sophomore year in Dartmouth College, taught the Hanover Academy two terms during the Fall of 1848 and the Winter of 1848-49. He was a descendant of the distinguished Rev. Dr. Gad Hitchcock of the West Parish of Pembroke, now Hanson, while his maternal great-grandfather was Dr. Jeremiah Hall, who bought what was afterwards known as the Horace Collamore place in North Pembroke about 1748, and who was a distinguished physician in his day—a surgeon in the French and Indian war, 1758, a member of the Provincial Congress in 1774, and a col-

CHARLES HITCHCOCK.

onel in the Revolutionary War. Mr. Hitchcock, the son of Charles and Abigail Little (Hall) Hitchcock, was born in Hanson, April 4, 1827 (though his parents afterwards lived in Pembroke) studied at the same time with myself and later in the Hanover Academy under Mr. Holmes, afterwards, in 1846, entered Phillips Andover Academy, graduated at Dartmouth college 1851, read law with Hon. Daniel Blaisdell, at

Hanover, N. H., one year, and then taught the classics a year in Washington, D. C. In the fall of 1853, he entered the senior class of the Dane Law School, at Cambridge, but finished for the bar with Harvey Jewell at Boston. In October, 1854, he began practice in Chicago where, during a professional service of many years, he came to be regarded as one of the foremost lawyers of the place. A Memorial of him, printed but not published, has been placed in my hands, and surely, if it be a just memorial, no one could desire higher testimonials of character and worth than were rendered to his memory by eminent members of the Bench and Bar, and by officers of the Historical Society. On July 10, 1860, he married Annie, daughter of James McClare, at Chicago, and he died in that city, May 6, 1881, leaving no children. For some years he was troubled with a distressing affection of the heart, for which he sought relief by going to Europe, but no curative influences from abroad, and no skill of physicians could remove or even alleviate the malady.

I may here add that his sister Sarah, who after teaching a brief space early passed away, and a younger brother, Bailey H. Hitchcock, also attended the Academy at the same time with myself. Bailey married an academy pupil, Sarah Collamore of N. Pembroke, and has made Toledo, Ohio, his home for more than forty years. He has one daughter, Mrs. A. C. Bartlett, and two sons. From a letter received from him, I learn that he has done work as civil engineer in more than ten states and in Canada.

GEORGE THEODORE WOLCOTT (1849) the son of Rev. Calvin Wolcott, was born in Hanover July 15, 1827.

was for two years in Brown University, where he graduated in 1848, taught here in Hanover one term in 1849, and died Oct. 22, 1851, in Quincy, and his remains were interred in the old Weymouth burying ground. He was never married.

The following letter from him to his brother, dated June 7, 1849, is interesting as showing his views and feelings, on his re-visiting for a while the scenes of his childhood:

"To-day there is a grand ship-launch at the lower yard, and I have given the school a half-holiday on the occasion. There is as much excitement among the juveniles of the present day at such a time, as there used to be of yore. They turn out *in toto* and throng the roads, and the Rainbow path, and sport along with the same glee as their predecessors of a former generation. . . .

"Everything about the village is now most pleasant and delightful. I know of no country village in New England more agreeable for a summer residence than Hanover. The trees are now almost in full leaf, the air is delightfully pure, mild and fragrant, and as you go out on an evening stroll, you are saluted with the varied songs of thousands (?!) of tuneful birds. There are so many delightful walks in every direction, over fields and through the woods, that one need never be tired of exploring them. I think the place has improved much lately. Mr. Cutler has had a good influence upon the people in the matter of taste,—setting out shade trees, &c."

He then speaks of the auction sale of "our old place" to Dr. Joseph B. Fobes, and almost wishes that his father had bought it. "The orchard," he says, "is one of the finest in the county. The trees which father set out have nearly attained their full size—very large and beautiful. Last week the orchard on the lane was almost one dense mass of blossoms, and the fragrance was perceptible at the Corners. . . . .

"I have had the school-room papered, and intend to get it painted soon. My school is increasing quite fast. It is a vacation at present in the Young Ladies' Seminary, up stairs."

Why Mr. Wolcott left the school after one term when everything seemed going on so prosperously, is explained by the fact that, in consequence of a severe cold he took when in college, the disease of consumption began to develop itself, and he took refuge during the following Winter in the milder climate of Virginia. But the end of earth for him was approaching, and in about two years after his teaching he was called up to a higher school.

In the Autumn of 1847, Miss MARY F. TAGGARD opened a school for young ladies in the upper hall of the Academy, and continued to teach there for some four years. She was the daughter of Mr. John Taggard of Charlestown, with whose business firm Mr. John Sylvester of Hanover was at one time connected. After leaving here she became the wife of Rev. Thomas Womersley, a native of England, who first studied medicine and afterwards graduated at Newton Theological Institution. After several years of preaching service, he returned to the practice of medicine, and finally died at Watertown, March, 1897.

A letter recently received from her recalls so vividly the past that we hesitate not to give it to our readers:

"The Young Ladies' Seminary began existence in the

Autumn of 1847, under the auspices of four residents of Hanover 'Four Corners,' each having one or more daughters of school age. The manager was Capt. John Cushing; the only teacher was Mary F. Taggard of Somerville. Outside pupils were admitted, not exceeding twenty in number. The upper floor of an old Academy building was a very pleasant school-room with ante-rooms—the lower floor being used for a boys' school. An old-style box-stove occupied the centre, a *standing* desk and an excellent piano were at one end, and a semi-circle of all that were fairest and dearest from the village occupied convenient seats with desks and other furnishings. There were happy times there. The teacher was but eighteen years of age, the scholars not far from the same, several of them older. There was an unusual degree of sympathy manifested; much interest in the studies which ranged pretty high for those days—and almost no friction in the discipline. The grave and quiet Mary Salmond, the studious Lizzie Waterman, Agnes Talbot, Josephine Josselyn, the tall daughters of Rev. Mr. Duncan, among the older,— Sarah Cushing, brimful of energy, the sweet little Barstow girls, the vivacious Eliza Smith Salmond among the younger pupils, are remembered as if I led them but yesterday. Every session began with Bible-reading and prayer. How well do I recall the village church, the sociables, the singers' gallery from which we had a full view of the great Daniel Webster as he came down the aisle every Sunday [occasionally, rather?] having driven over from his Marshfield residence—the Sabbath school, the Wednesday evening services. . . .

Of the boys' school below, Mr. Wolcott, and then Mr. McLauthlin, was Principal. George R. Dwelley, a pupil there at that time, has been Superintendent of our Watertown schools for, I think, a score or more of years and has just resigned here," &c.

The following is a list (as written at the time, by one of the pupils, E. T. W.,) of young ladies whom she taught in 1849:

"Maria E. Soule, Mary Salmond, Sarah Briggs, Elizabeth T. Waterman, Elizabeth Ramsdell, Sophia B. Loring, Agnes H. Talbot, Mary E. Torrey, Maria C. Josselyn, Huldah B. Dwelley, Sarah E. Cushing, Emma Barstow, Lydia C. Pratt, Lucy A. Barstow, Mary E. Barstow, Ruth M. Eels, Huldah M. Stetson, Eliza A. Josselyn, Ruth W. Stetson, Mary A. Stetson, Laura J. Duncan, Lucia A. Duncan, Annie L. Eells, Maria W. Wright, Susan Turner."

Perhaps nearly a majority of these are with us to this day, and the married ones are doubtless the pride and boast of their husbands and children. We leave Daniel E. Damon, William Carver Bates, and others personally interested, to supply the rest of the chapter.

Mr. Martin Parris McLauthlin (1850-54) was born in Duxbury, July 24, 1825, and was the son of Martin McLauthlin and Hannah Howard Reed, daughter of the distinguished inventor, Col. Jesse Reed of Marshfield. The family early moving to E. Bridgewater, he attended the Bridgewater academies and then went to Phillips Andover Academy, where he graduated from the classical department in 1847. After teaching the Winter term, 1849-50 of the Grammar school at North Marshfield, now Marshfield Hills, he became the Principal of Hanover Academy, beginning his service March, 1850, and ending it in February, 1854, when he engaged in business with his brother. Under his tuition the Academy attained a very high degree of prosperity.

On April 10, 1860, Mr. McLauthlin married Elizabeth Pease Vincent, second daughter of the Hon. Ambrose and Susan (Parker) Vincent of New Bedford, and settled upon his father's homestead in E. Bridgewater, where

MARTIN PARRIS McLAUTHLIN.

all his children, six in number, were born. He now resides in Malden, where his wife died Nov. 22, 1890, leaving five children. Besides this loss he has met with other severe affliction. In Aug. 14, 1892, his eldest son, George Vincent, who was an instructor in Biology in the Mass. Institute of Technology, from which he graduated in 1888, died from drowning at Nahant, aged 24. Another son, Parker Reed, born Nov. 22, 1877, died April 23d, 1896, being at the time a member of the above Institute. The other surviving children are Elizabeth Rena, Martin Bernard, and Sara Louise. The son on June 1, 1898, married Miss Grace C. Grant, and lives in Malden.

For the first two years Mr. McLauthlin taught in the old or second Academy, after which the building was sold to Mr. Hiram Randall for $375, and moved some years afterward to High street, Pembroke, where it was used for a carriage and paint shop. Subsequently a third story was added to the building, and it now bears the name of Mechanics' Hall. We think that much good work was done in that building while it stood at Hanover Four Corners.

As illustrative of the culture received here in those early days, we give the following incident as related by a correspondent, the initials of whose name we will give as A. B. C.

"I was making a journey by rail in another State when a gentleman came in with three bright little girls and took a seat near me. I was attracted by their appearance and soon we got acquainted, and engaged in an animated conversation, told stories, etc. The father was a silent listener for a while, then said to me rather abruptly, 'Will you please tell me where you were educated? I am engaged in literary work, and your language seems so spontaneous and correct, and so different from the present style of conglomeration, I was in hopes you were a teacher somewhere that I might send my girls to be educated.' I said I received most, I might say all, my education in a small country Academy. He said, 'Is it still in existence, and teaching on the old lines?' I said, 'It is still there, but modernized to suit the times.' 'What a pity!' said he; 'those old academical institutions have sent out more real, practical students than all our modern colleges and famous scientific schools. Then only *students* studied, because they desired knowledge for its worth ; now half the time is wasted just to kill it.' " We leave our readers to pass their own judgment on the above, and to draw their own inferences.

PART III.
HANOVER ACADEMY, 1852-92.
Its Third Building and its Teachers.*

THE THIRD BUILDING.

*For the above picture I am indebted to Mr. A. E. Foss of Needham, publisher of the Rockland and Hanover Directory.

As Mr. McLauthlin was the last teacher in the old Academy, so he was the first teacher in the new, and was indeed greatly efficient in bringing about the erection of the latter building. This edifice, much more pretentious in appearance than the former ones, stands some fifteen rods back from the street and from where the old Academy stood, on a high and beautiful elevation of land which commands an extensive and fine prospect. This said parcel of land, containing one acre, " be the same more or less," was purchased in 1851 of Capt. Nathan Dwelley and wife, who deeded it to forty-three grantees, including two societies, all whose names are seven times written in full in the deed, and once with the proportion paid by each.* It was paid for in shares amounting to 105 in number, at $1.66 1-2 per share, Samuel Salmond, Esq., heading the list with forty-two shares taken. The following is an abstract of the Deed:

Know all men by these Presents that I, Nathan Dwelley, of Hanover, etc., and I, Huldah B. Dwelley, wife of said Nathan, in my right, in consideration of $175, to me paid by Samuel Salmond, Robert Sylvester, Seth Barker, Frances Baldwin, Alexander Wood, Gustavus Percival, Stephen Josselyn, Thomas B. Donnell, Hannah Barstow, Charles Dyer, Robert Hersey, Martin W. Stetson, Hannah Stetson, John P. Eells, Benjamin Whitwell, John Sylvester, Nathaniel Barstow, Benjamin F. Burgess, Martin P. McLauthlin, Michael Sylvester,

---

*Among these grantees were six individuals, Alexander Wood, Nathaniel Barstow, John B. Barstow, Thomas Waterman, Haviland Torrey and Luther Howland, who were original stockholders in the old Academy. Of these same grantees three only are now living, Robert Sylvester, Robert E. Dwelley, and M. P. McLauthlin.

George Curtis, Warren Wright, Joseph B. Fobes, Edmund Q. Sylvester, Robert E. Dwelley, William Church, Nathan Dwelley, John B. Barstow, Samuel Cutler, as Rector of St. Andrew's Church, of Hanover aforesaid, and by Samuel Cutler in behalf of the Dorcas Society of said St. Andrew's Church, and also by the said Samuel Cutler in behalf of the Young Ladies' Society of said St. Andrew's Church, all of Hanover in said County of Plymouth; and Elijah Barstow, Isaac H. Haskins, Abner Stetson, Thomas Waterman, Samuel Tolman, Jr., Lemuel C. Waterman, Josiah M. Smith, and George P. Clapp of South Scituate in the County of Plymouth, aforesaid ; and Levi Sturtevant, Jr., Haviland Torrey and Adam Billings of Pembroke in said County, and Luther Howland, of Hanson in said County, the receipt whereof is hereby acknowledged, do hereby give, grant, bargain, sell, and convey unto the said (Salmond and others) a certain piece of woodland lying near the Four Corners, so called, in said Hanover, containing one acre and bounded as follows . . . . . or however otherwise bounded—to them and to their heirs or successors forever ; reserving to myself and to my heirs or assigns the right of passing and repassing the same—hereby also granting a passage from said above granted premises to the highway leading from said Four Corners in said Hanover to Bridgewater, 40 feet wide, with a full and perfect right of occupancy of the same, for and during the time that the before granted premises shall be improved for a school, —and the above named grantees hereby bind themselves and their successors to erect and maintain around said granted premises a good and substantial picket fence, supported by stone posts—and the said grantees further bind themselves and their heirs or successors that the land of said Nathan and Huldah B. Dwelley adjoining the above granted premises shall not be injured or in any manner trespassed upon by the occupants of the above granted premises, and the said grantees yet further bind themselves and their heirs or successors that nothing of a sectarian nature shall pertain to the above said school.

To have and to hold the above granted premises with the privileges and appurtenances thereto belonging to them the said (Salmond and others), their heirs and assigns to their use and behoof forever.

And the said grantors do covenant with the said (Salmond and others) that we are lawfully seized in fee of the afore granted premises, that they are free from all incumbrances, that we have good right to sell and convey the same to the said (Salmond and others), and that we will and our heirs, Executors and Administrators shall Warrant and Defend the same to the said (Salmond and others), their heirs and assigns forever against the lawful claims and demands of all persons.

The above deed, which was executed August 5, 1851, was written, presumably, by Alexander Wood, Esq., of Hanover, but was acknowledged before Col. Samuel Tolman, of South Scituate, as Justice of the Peace. On November 20th, 1852, it was received and recorded in the Registry of Deeds, Book 249, Pages 98, 99, 100. William S. Russell, Register.

A contract for building the Academy, fencing the grounds and digging a well, was made with Robert E. Dwelley for the sum of $2240. The digging of a cellar for wood-room, etc., was not in the original contract, and of course was an extra expense. There was paid to

Nathan Dwelley for six-ninths of the old Academy, $300, and to Samuel Salmond, Haviland Torrey, and J. B. Barstow, who each owned one-ninth, $150. A bell costing $138, was given by Mary Salmond, eldest daughter of Samuel Salmond. Including these items we find the total cost of the buildings and grounds as furnished and prepared to be $3483.52, which sum was paid for in 110 shares, at $25 per share, together with individual subscriptions, donations from the Young Ladies' Society, and proceeds from the sale of the old Academy. All the grantees mentioned in the Deed, and four others, T. H. C. Barstow, Rev. Abel G. Duncan, Dr. A. C. Garratt, and Melzar Hatch, who by paying $25 each, and by signing the Constitution and By-laws became entitled " to all the rights and privileges of proprietors," took shares in the same—Mr. Salmond heading the list with 42 shares taken. Taking into account all that Mr. Salmond and family did for this new building and subsequently for the school, we think it might have been properly named the Salmond Academy.*

The school was kept in the lower part of the building, while the upper hall was early furnished with a carpet, settees, curtain fixtures, etc. By formal vote the building was to be used only for " educational, moral and lit-

*On occasion of the death of Mr. Salmond, May 28th, 1859, the Trustees passed the following Resolve :
"As a benefactor and a practical advocate of education he was deservedly esteemed by this community. His demise, while a public loss, is more particularly a loss to education and religion, and while the dispensation of Providence is a subject of regret to the friends of the Academy, they bear a grateful testimonial to his unfeigned liberality." A subsequent teacher, Mr. Conant, in a letter recently received, says, "Had it not been for his (Mr. Salmond's) help, his influence, and his willing, earnest daughter, I hardly think the new Academy would have been built."

Eliza Salmond.

erary purposes, purely and unquestionably as such." Subsequently its uses were enlarged, and a considerable income was derived therefrom. It has been rented to the Episcopal, Congregational and Methodist Societies for religious services, sewing circles, fairs, festivals, etc., and once, in 1860, for a " Friends' Meeting ; " also for divers exhibitions, concerts, singing schools, gymnastic class. Brass band, Lyceum, panoramic shows, flower shows, divers lectures on education, temperance, phrenology, politics (including one Kansas meeting) and once at least to "Comical Brown."

The most noted assemblage that ever gathered in the upper hall was at the dedication of the Soldiers' Monument, July 17, 1878, when a carload of dignitaries arrived from Boston, including Governor Rice, Speaker Long, General Banks, Secretary Pierce, and many others, all of whom repaired thither to partake of "a substantial and inviting breakfast provided by the generous hospitality of the ladies of the venerable parish of St. Andrew." (See Dedication Pamphlet, pp 9, 10). We may here also state that many of the most distinguished orators of the day have given lectures in the Hall under the auspices of the Lyceum Club, of which we may speak further on.

On Sept, 22, 1851, a Constitution and By-laws as prepared chiefly by Mr McLauthlin were adopted, under which constitution, early the next year, the following Board of Trustees were elected : Samuel Salmond, Esq., Rev. Samuel Cutler, Rev. Abel G. Duncan, Dr. Alfred C. Garratt, Seth Barker, Capt. Elijah Barstow and M. P. McLauthlin, *ex officio.*

On Sept. 29, Mr. McLauthlin, Charles Dyer, and Rev. Samuel Cutler were appointed "a Committee to prepare, if they think it expedient, for the dedication of the New Academy."

The printed ORDER OF EXERCISES as prepared by the Committee reads as follows :

DEDICATION OF

HANOVER ACADEMY.

Hanover, Mass.,

On Tuesday, March 2, 1852, at 2 o'clock, P. M.

Voluntary.

Invocatory Prayer, by Rev. A. G. Duncan.

HYMN.
By Miss Lucy S. Delano.

Why meet we here, a happy band?
　Within these new-raised walls,
Erected by the artists' hand,
　Whose touch the forest falls.

We've come to dedicate a shrine,
　To fill with richest lore ;
Where truth and purity may shine,
　And wisdom's depths explore.

And here let little children come
　Secure from all that harms,
Drawn gently, as the Holy One
　Once called them to His arms.

Thy blessing, Father, on us here,
　Thy favor each would share ;
Teachers and children, without fear,
　We give unto Thy care.

Dedicatory Address, by Rev. E. Porter Dyer.

Dedicatory Prayer, by Rev. Samuel Cutler.

HYMN.

By Rev. E. Porter Dyer.

The Pilgrim left his native land
    A thousand leagues behind,
In drear New England's wilderness
    A dwelling place to find.
He came in faith across the sea,
    And lo! the desert smiled;
A meeting-house he built for self,
    A school-house for his child.

For well he knew his sturdy faith,
    Bequeathed unto his heir,
Would flourish in a cultured soil
    The best of any where.
He therefore eschewed ignorance,
    And planted Learning's tree,
Among whose glorious later fruits
    Stands our ACADEMY.

Then hail the day which bids us meet
    With services Divine,
To consecrate to Learning's self,
    Another graceful shrine;
Where Science leagued with Literature,
    May shed a cheerful ray
On generations that shall rise,
    When we are passed away.

And distant be the woful hour,
    The period long remote,
Ere Time or Flame these beauteous walls
    To ruin shall devote.
Meanwhile, be theirs the rich reward,
    Who reared this classic dome,
That literature and science here,
    Have found a pleasing home.

ADDRESSES.

HYMN.

By Rev. A. G. Duncan.

Lord, our God, Thy wondrous glory,
    In our song we celebrate;

Not for fields with carnage gory,
　Won from foes in deadly hate,
　　But for peaceful
　Fruits, that now we dedicate.

Thanks we give, and seek Thy blessing
　On our humble enterprise;
In Thy ways still onward pressing,
　In Thy wisdom we are wise.
　　Strong and faithful
　Make us, as we higher rise.

For Thy glory, may this building
　Learning's favored temple stand,
With a gushing fountain yielding
　Streams to gladden e'er each band
　　Gathering hither,
　Youth! the hope of Freedom's land.

On th' immortal leaves, unfolding,
　Of the youthful mind and heart,
Be inscribed bright lines for moulding
　By fair virtue's heavenly art,
　　Youthful genius,
　In Thy cause to act its part.

BENEDICTION.

We here subjoin Mr. Dyer's Address, which, according to the Records, was published by request and paid for by subscription. The author in a Prefatory note says: "This Address was written and delivered without a thought on my part that a copy of it would ever be required for the press."

" LADIES AND GENTLEMEN :—The occasion which has brought us together in this place and at this hour, is an occasion of no ordinary interest.

We are assembled to set apart and dedicate this House, with becoming religious services, to the purposes of sound learning and instruction.

In compliance with an invitation from the Committee of Proprietors, I appear before you to offer, in connection with these services, a brief Introductory Address.

Sincerely do I regret, as I have often regretted since accepting the invitation, that this duty had not devolved on some abler and better man, who, if not a more ardent friend of the Cause of Sound Learning than I am, might, nevertheless, be more thoroughly posted up in the unwritten history of modern Education, and every way better able to add to the exercises of this occasion a becoming charm.

But I stand before you with a heart deeply impressed with the importance of sound learning. And sincerely do I rejoice with you in the blessing which, after so much of deliberation and anxiety and effort and cost, has at length crowned your enterprise with such abundant success.

In my judgment it is no light thing to assume the responsibility of developing and moulding the intellectual character of a single pupil. It is no slight blessing conferred on an individual, on society, on the world, when that individual is thoroughly educated and fitted to occupy as a citizen of the world, positions of responsibility and trust. The man who takes up one such individual, though a lad from the streets, and educates and gives him to the world, becomes a benefactor of his race. What then must be the richness and extent of that manifold blessing which confers an education on the whole neighborhood and of an entire generation. But your work contemplates blessing not one neighborhood alone, but many. The structure you have reared is substantial. You expect the feet of more than one generation of youths will cross its threshold to obtain instruction within its consecrated walls. And doubtless, long after most of you who have been deeply interested and actively engaged in its erection, shall have been gathered to your fathers, this noble edifice, standing where you have reared it, and proffering the advantages of an Academic Education to all, will welcome to its halls a multitude of those who shall come after you on the journey of life. Your children's children will eat the fruit of the tree you have planted, and sit down under its shadow with great delight And this institution so cherished by you who have furnished to learning this beautiful asylum, will exert on this community its enlightening, elevating, refining influences, possibly till *they* themselves shall cease to be any longer interested in all that is done under the sun.

Not without design, then, stands this elegant structure here. It was erected for a specific purpose. To that purpose it is to be publicly set apart and consecrated to-day. That we may be the better prepared to engage in this service, let us consider a moment

The purpose of its erection, and—

The manner in which that purpose is expected to be accomplished.

FIRST. To what purpose has this house been erected? Certainly not to become a sacred fane, with its mitred priest and its altar, whereon incense shall be religiously offered to the Most High, and where the tenets of some particular religious sect shall be sedulously inculcated, as if life and death depended on the ability to pronounce some denominational Shibboleth; not to become an arena for the hot discussion of political creeds with a view to preoccupy with preferences and prejudices the minds of pupils, deafening their young ears with the everlasting din of party politics.

Nor yet was it reared as a princely palace to Mammon, to add one more to the ten thousand superb Plutian temples, which, for selfish ends, private enterprise is erecting all over the land to the God of riches.

And yet it is gravely hinted in some quarters that an American citizen cares only for three things—Religion, Politics, Money—and that his whole soul is intent on reaching the summit of this inverted climax. It is intimated that he prizes his religion mainly for the liberty it gives him to go into politics with individual earnestness, and a delightful consciousness of his inherent dignity as one of the sovereign people; that he loves his politics only as they open to him one chance in ten thousand of securing some lucrative office or some pecuniary reward which shall enable him more luxuriously to feast his greedy eyes on gold, or lay on the altar of his devout worship one fresh token of his affection for his heart's dearest idol which he has irreverently denominated the "Almighty Dollar."

But though there be too much truth in this severe insinuation, we rejoice to believe it is not wholly true. Here stands a noble edifice which measurably contradicts the foul aspersion—which speaks to the passing traveller, and which will continue to speak to generations to come, the delightful fact, that, however as Americans we may in general regard the peculiarities of our respective religious sects, however we may cultivate our zeal for party politics, and cherish our insatiable love of silver and of gold, there are among us men of too much discernment, of too much shrewd prophetic forecast, not to know that if we exhaust all our energies on these hobbies, the inheritance we shall transmit to our children will be poor indeed. And it is delightful to see men acting under this salutary conviction. It is delightful to see them at times laying aside their denominational and party distinctions for the general good. It is delightful to see them casting their money into a common treasury, uniting heart and hand in extending, as you now do, to the children of successive generations a cordial welcome to the blessings of wholesome mental discipline and sound learning.

Thus far, on this point, I have spoken somewhat negatively. I have said the purpose for which this house is erected is not specifically for religion, politics, nor pecuniary gain. But it is designed to be a temple of Education, and Education in this use of the term contemplates the mind of youth in a two-fold aspect.

1st. As a treasure-house of knowledge. God has endowed every rational mind with a capacity for knowledge, and a faculty of retaining it. In the aged person, this faculty, strengthened by exercise, often attains to a capaciousness that is truly wonderful. His memory may have lost something of its retentive power, and yet it is capacious and full. The old revolutionary hero can draw from the recollections of the past many a thrilling incident, unwind many a thread of history, for his memory is as full of "long yarns" as a cocoon is of silken fibres. The new-born intellect of the child, however, is undeveloped. In him the capacity of memory is yet limited. It demands expansion. In him curiosity is awake. Whatever arrests his attention is stored in his memory. And the more he treasures there the more does he strengthen memory and increase its capacity.

Now, to direct the curiosity and fix the attention of

youth upon those facts and events in History, those axioms and principles in Science and Philosophy, which shall hereafter be esteemed acquisitions of no small value, but which on the contrary shall serve to guide the active powers of the mind, is one very important branch of the business of Education, and regarding Education as a distinct science this seems to be one of its fundamental principles, *viz.*, to preoccupy the mind as early as possible with that which shall be of the greatest service in riper years.

It is recorded of Agesilaus, king of Sparta, that, on being asked what he thought most proper for boys to learn, he replied, " That which they will need most when they come to be men."

In accordance with this just remark you have provided here a commodious house where the elements of science and literature may be taught, and where the foundation may be begun for future intelligence and even for eminent learning. For, alas! to educate the mind as a store-house and to do it *thoroughly*, is beyond the power of any institution of learning in the land. This must be the work of a lifetime, if, indeed, human life itself be not a period too short—a work which is thorough and complete only when the mind is actually full and incapable of any further progress or expansion forever. The foundation of this great work, however, as I have already said, may be begun here. To this purpose then, as a part of the object contemplated in its erection, we dedicate this beautiful Academy. Day after day, week after week, term after term, year after year, as pupils go down to their respective homes from this seat of learning, may it be with their minds rendered more capacious as store-houses, and not only more capacious, but more abundantly enriched with the treasures of wisdom and knowledge than when they came up hither. Here may the principles of Astronomy, of Botany, of Chemistry, of Declamation, of Elocution, of Geography, and so on through the whole alphabet of science and literature, be treasured in their minds. I say the principles ; for these are very few, though the facts arranged under any one of them may be innumerable. Take, for instance, " The Rule of Three ;" the principle is simple, easy to be comprehended, easy to be retained. The cases that might occur under this principle, however, are without number. We ask not that the mind be burdened with such cases, but only with the principle, which with ordinary mental discipline can always be applied as occasion demands. To fix these general principles in a pupil's mind is, I repeat it, an important part of the business of Education.

2d. Education further contemplates the mind of youth as an agent or instrument.

It is evident, however much a man may know, his knowledge can be of no essential benefit to the world if he has no faculty of communicating what he knows. Hence Education contemplates the mind, not merely as the passive recipient, but also as the active dispenser of knowledge, as an instrument, or rather a case of instruments, all of which need to be ground and set to the keenest possible edge, that the owner may have them always at hand, all sharp, keen, bright, and ready for use at a moment's warning. Take, for instance the faculty of Reason. It needs to be so developed, strengthened and trained by exercise, as to be ready to discuss and argue debatable questions, and be ever able to deduce just inferences from given premises. To discipline the faculty of Reason into such perfection of skill as to enable him to do all this with the greatest promptness, precision and ease is one of the proudest triumphs of Education.

Take the faculty of Imagination. Its province is, out of ideas previously stored in the mind, to form such striking combinations as never before existed ; such as excite wonder and admiration in the poems of Byron, the plans of Napoleon, or the novels of Scott; such as you discover with rare delight in the creations of the artist's pencil, or in the musical compositions of a Handel or a Mozart. The teacher may not know which of his pupils or whether any of them will gain celebrity by the productions of his imagination ; and yet the cultivation of this faculty, so as to render it quick and skilful at combinations, and ready for invention, is part of the business of Education. And so it is with regard to all the active intellectual powers.

I need not stop here to point out the precise benefits which may accrue to each faculty of the mind by education. But I must say this, that while Education aims to store the mind with facts and principles, it also aims so to discipline its powers as to render that mind a fitter instrument for the production of knowledge. It is important not merely that a pupil acquire knowledge, but that he also receive such mental culture as shall enable him to make the best use of his knowledge and secure the greatest amount of power and influence for good with his fellow citizens. Hence he must learn not only what in literature and science is important to be known, but also the art of writing and speaking according to the established rules of Logic, Rhetoric and Grammar.

that he may both easily and impressively communicate to others the results of his own observations or reflections.

These things are perfectly obvious. How inestimable must be the blessings conferred by such an education.

SECOND. But in what manner or by what means is it expected that these blessings are to be secured here?

The answer to this inquiry is brief. You have erected here a spacious, elegant temple, which we now consecrate to educational purposes. If it be not already done you will doubtless, sooner or later, find it desirable to furnish this Academy with some convenient school apparatus for illustrating the different branches of science taught here. But neither this beautiful house, nor any amount of instrumental furniture will of itself educate one of your children, if, having provided these, you keep the doors locked and your children at home. Nor will your children become educated by going to an Academy, however splendid the building, or however richly endowed, unless you have stationed there, to greet them when they come, and instruct them while they remain, one who has not only drunk deep at the fountains of knowledge himself, but who possesses that happy faculty of communicating his knowledge which shall both interest and benefit his pupils. Such teachers it is not always an easy matter to procure. But when such an one is secured, as I understand is the case among you, remember, I pray you, that even *he* cannot labor to the greatest advantage without your continual support and sympathy, your friendly counsel and encouragement. Nay, in the same breath in which you ask God to bless your beloved children, ask him to bless also your Academy, that it may become a nursery not of education alone, but of piety and virtue; and plead especially for him who is daily making his mark on the minds of your sons and daughters, that he may fulfil the high responsibilities of his office as "a workman that needeth not to be ashamed."

For such purposes then, to be secured by such means was this house erected. To such purposes we now sacredly dedicate it in the name and behalf of the Proprietors.

Gentlemen of the Trustees: You have been chosen to guard the interests of this institution and to secure this edifice so far as in you lies, for the purposes for which it was built. We congratulate you that Literature and Science, having long enjoyed here a temporary dwelling-place, have at last consented to be installed in this new temple, under your guardianship, and to make this a permanent abode.

And, fellow-citizens, as friends of Education and lovers of our race, from this elevated standpoint, we cannot help casting our eye down the long vista of the future to contemplate the blessings which will flow from this humble seat of learning to generations yet unborn. When we think of the number of eminent men and distinguished women who shall hereafter look back and point with mingled pride and veneration to this consecrated spot, we cannot but hail this as a proud day for Hanover. It is not among the least-pleasing circumstances of this hour to learn that this is wholly a popular enterprise; that the stock of this house, divided into small shares, has, for the most part, been taken by your citizens, that the thing might be the creation of the people. I am pleased to learn that a liberal donation of one thousand dollars, towards the erection of this building, has been cheerfully made by one of the venerable fathers of the town to whom God has given both the means and a heart for this service. Nor did it afford me any less pleasure to learn that a benevolent lady among you has also made a generous donation to endow what, for want of a better title, I may denominate a sort of Belfry Professorship, in the department of Punctuality; and that through her beneficence, you have been enabled already to secure for that important Professorship the services of a "tonguey fellow," of striking and persuasive eloquence, who without much knowledge of any *science* in particular, is nevertheless thoroughly versed in BELL-LETTERS.

All these agreeable circumstances add to this hour a delightful charm. Once more, then, before we separate, let us join heart and voice in the consecration of this beautiful Edifice. To SCIENCE, LITERATURE, EDUCATION, we now consecrate these halls, these seats, these desks, these walls. May the Lord God of our Fathers smile on this humble effort of their children, to transmit the blessings of knowledge through this Academy to multitudes unborn.

While I am speaking the cry for educated men is waxing louder and louder. It is coming up from the four quarters of the globe, from every department of human industry. A few years ago if the learned professions, so called, were supplied with men of thorough education, it was enough. Now our teachers, our public lecturers, our school committees, our engineers, our mechanics, our farmers, are calling for, nay, loudly demanding, that more of the genial light of science be shed on their respective pursuits and callings. And these demands must be met. And happy is that people who, yearning for the welfare of their race, and admonished by those "coming events" which "cast their shadows before," have anticipated the increasing demand for the general diffusion of learning, and have stepped forth to do their part toward supplying the demand, as we deem it no flattery to say, you have *nobly done yours.*

The following account of the Dedicatory Exercises taken from the Hingham Journal, signed D., was without doubt written by Rev. Mr. Dyer.*

"*Messrs Editors:* I herewith enclose you a copy of the Order of Exercises at the Dedication of Hanover Academy. This new, neat, commodious, and, withal, beautiful, building was dedicated on Tuesday last with appropriate religious services. Notwithstanding the storm, the hall, which is judged capable of seating three hundred, was well filled. Many ladies were present. Instead of a voluntary, as the storm prevented the bringing in of an instrument for that purpose, the Choir [under the direction of Mr. Benjamin Frost] favored us with an Anthem for an opening exercise. Then followed an Invocatory Prayer, by Rev. A. G. Duncan; Hymn by Miss Lucy S. Delano of Scituate; Dedicatory Address, by Rev. E. Porter Dyer, of Hingham; Dedicatory Prayer, by Rev. Samuel Cutler, of Hanover; Hymn, by Rev. E. Porter Dyer.

A very interesting letter from Rev. Lucius Alden,

---

*Mr. Dyer was born in So. Abington (Whitman) in 1813. Graduated at Brown University, 1833, and was pastor in Hingham some sixteen years, resigning in 1864. In his last years he supplied the Congregational church at Hanover Corners until 1881, when he was laid aside by paralysis and died at So. Abington the next year.

formerly a pupil at Hanover Academy—a letter running back to its foundation, and glancing at its history for many years, speaking of men who had gone forth from that Academy and acquired some celebrity, being read by the Principal of the Academy, was well received, and furnished appropriate topics for subsequent remark. Addresses were then made by Rev. Messrs. Walker and White of Abington, Rev. Mr. Slason, of Hanover, and Mr. M. P. McLauthlin, the Principal. A Hymn, by Rev. A. G. Duncan was then sung, and the exercises closed with Benediction by Rev. Mr. Slason. It was said that several clergymen from neighboring towns were invited who were not present, probably on account of the storm.

It is now about half a century since the Academy in Hanover was founded, and we congratulate the citizens of that town that this long cherished institution in their midst is thus furnished with a new building at a cost of some three thousand dollars. This new edifice stands in a beautiful young grove directly in rear of the old building; it is painted white, and furnished with green blinds and a tower, and makes quite an imposing appearance. The bell, weighing four hundred pounds, was the gift of a young lady in Hanover. — Yours respectfully."

In the pamphlet containing the Address, the Trustees —Rev. Samuel Cutler, President—add the following :

The occasion of the dedication of the new Academy seems to bespeak auspicious omens in regard to the future prosperity of the Institution, as under the well-devised and energetic action of Samuel Salmond, Esq., seconded by the cordial unanimity of many others interested, there has been effected a new organization of the Academy, by the adoption of a regular Constitution and the establishment of an elective Board of Trustees, by which a permanent direction might be given to the school, independent of sectarian prejudices, yet by no means void of a strong and healthful moral government.

The Trustees and Proprietors of the Institution also fondly anticipate that, through a continued, as far as may be, and effective Principal as the chief Instructor, by which the school may be devoid of an oscillating character, the Institution may enjoy the ready confidence of the public and attain a worthy eminence. The new and elegant Academy, together with its ample grounds, is pleasantly situated on rather a commanding site, being retired some distance from the street. It is commodiously constructed, in accordance with the modern style. . . . . The Fall Term will commence about the last of September and continue eleven weeks.

SIGNED BY THE TRUSTEES.

Mr. McLauthlin continued as the first teacher in the new Academy until Feb., 1854. He thinks the largest number that attended any one term was sixty. According to the Records, he was granted, in Feb. 9, 1853, for reasons not stated, "leave of absence for three months — he retaining his position as Principal of the school and supplying Mr. Frederic O. Barstow to take his place during his absence." On the occasion of his resigning the Principalship, the Trustees express their sense of the importance of his labors as a teacher, especially, perhaps, as connected with the building of the new Academy, in these words: "Resolved, That the Trustees of the Hanover Academy hereby accept the resignation of Mr. M. P. McLauthlin, and tender to him their thanks for his zeal, energy and fidelity as Principal of the Academy, and express their desires for his future usefulness and happiness."

There is no full list of Mr. McLauthlin's scholars. Many of Mr. Holmes' pupils, as those of Messrs. Hitchcock and Wolcott, doubtless continued to study under this teacher. The following names have not, I think, been mentioned before, and perhaps most of these were new scholars. I trust no one will look for perfection in these partly conjectural lists which follow, or blame me for any want of accuracy. I should the rather be blamed for attempting the impossible.

The names below which are asterisked will reappear in Mr. Conant's catalogue. Perhaps some of them should have made their first appearance in his list rather than here.

Sidney Barstow,* William Carver Bates,* Elmina Curtis, Sarah Collamore, Theodore Dyer, Jedediah Dwelley, Harriet L. Garratt,* Cyrus C. Holmes,* Sophia B. Loring, John E. Sylvester, Loammi B. Sylvester, Susanna F. Sylvester, Moses Bass Smith,* Alphonso L. Sturtevant, Edward P. Stetson, Mary A. Stetson, Benjamin Barstow Torrey,* Herbert Torrey* Zephaniah Talbot, Ebenezer C. Waterman.*

From a circular sent out some years since to the "Class of 1852," by Mr. L. Vernon Briggs, and from the replies thereto, I should infer that some of the following mainly new names might also belong here :

Melzar C. Bailey,* Charles B. Briggs,* Ara Brooks, Eliza M. Billings,* George C. Briggs,* John Corthell, Mary W. Curtis, Mary A. Church, Arabella Collamore, Caroline D. Collamore, Mary B. Church,* Sarah Collamore, Priscilla Ellis, Henry Hunt, Andrew Howland,

Franklin Jacobs, Caleb B. Josselyn, William C. Litchfield, Clara H. Mann, Susan M. Magoun,* John C. Nash,* George B. Oldham, Allen Phillips, Ruth C. Pratt, Cerena Pocorney, Joseph C. Stockbridge, Sarah J. Stetson, Cordelia Sherman, Frances Turner, Joanna Taylor, Lucy Vinal, Kilborn Whitman, Edward Whitman, Oren T. Whiting, Thomas Whiting, Cynthia Whiting, Tryphena Whiting, Ellen A. Wood.*

GEORGE CONANT.

MR. GEORGE CONANT, Principal, and MRS. MARY ANNE FRIEND CONANT, Assistant Teacher, (1854-55), began their first term March 13, 1854, with 42 scholars. Previous to his coming here he had been teaching for two years in Topsfield of this State. In the announcement for the Fall Term we learn that in the ladies' department instruction by the Preceptress was given not only in music on the Organ and Piano Forte, but also in Duo-Chromatic or two Crayon drawing, specimens of which (worth from five to a hundred dollars) could be seen at the Academy, resembling the finest steel engraving; Painting in water colors; wax flowers and fruit; worsted flowers and embroidery; and ornamental leather frames, in imitation of carved walnut. We also learn that a "Young Men's and Young Ladies' Literary Society for the purpose of Debate etc., is connected with the school, affording an excellent opportunity for self-improvement. A Library and an apparatus belong to the Society and School." This "Philomathean" Society and Library were founded in the last part of Mr. McLauthlin's administration, (the Library in Oct., 1853), and the Catalogue of books, which I have seen, numbers nearly three hundred. Many of these books were purchased, and many were donated by students and the teachers and by out-siders, of whom Mr. Salmond was by far the largest giver. The book which heads the list and marked No. 1, was Drake's Indian Chiefs, presented by William Carver Bates, a student at that time. The Library Book not only gives the names of the Books but also, from the year 1856, the names of the scholars or teachers who took them out, though with serious breaks, even as far down as the year 1865. This list shows a large number of names of whom no literary Institution need be ashamed. In our Academy Archives is preserved one green, faded, water-stained ribbon imprinted in large letters; PHILOMATHEAN SOCIETY.*

*Old Philomathea, the scene of debate—miniature house of Congress, save the Investigating Committee—many a night we decided there the destiny of nations, and no nation suffered at our hands.

A Lyceum Club, which was formed in the village when Mr. McLauthlin was teacher, seems to have been very flourishing under Mr. Conant's administration; and a Trustee's vote passed Oct., 1854, allows them to have the "use of the Academy Hall and fixtures for twelve evenings at .75 per evening." The course of Lectures during the Winter, the admittance fee to which was only ten cents, was largely attended, and among the list of speakers were Rev. John Pierpont, Judge Thomas Russell, Edwin P. Whipple, George S. Boutwell and Oliver Wendell Holmes. Such distinguished Lecturers as these were paid at the rate of from five to eight dollars apiece with their expenses, and they were obliged to ride in a cold stage-coach from Abington and return. To reach the first morning train to Boston they had to partake of breakfast before daylight. Now our lecturers can ride in palace or electric cars and get their one or two hundred dollars per lecture. It would be interesting could some one write the history of this club. I have been told that Rev. Dr. Ezra Gannett, Hon. Josiah Quincy, and others alike distinguished, lectured here in the previous Winter.

Under Mr. Conant's administration, in 1854 and 1855, large additions were made to the Philosophical apparatus of the Academy, amounting in value to $222. Of this sum Mr. Salmond paid $100, Messrs. Robert Sylvester, George Curtis, and John Cushing paid $10 each, Michael Sylvester and Elijah Barstow, $5 each, a lecture by Mr. Conant netted $6.60. The proceeds of an Exhibition, held Nov. 27--28, 1854, were $63.36; and

though proud Albion's Queen had good cause to protest against the cruel murder of the King's English.—C. C. Holmes, Newberne, N. C., Nov. 28, 1876.

the balance, twelve dollars, was made up by Mr. Salmond.

The admission fee to the above "Exhibition" was only ten cents, and the Academy Hall was crowded and jammed each evening. On the second evening, as Mr. Conant writes me, "the boys and girls outdid themselves. They were encored repeatedly, and kept the sweating and eager listeners in their seats and on their feet till about midnight." The exercises consisted mainly in the speaking of pieces and dialogues, and in singing. Of course the then famous "Box and Cox" was vividly acted out on the stage. One dialogue, entitled, "The Nervous Man and the Man of Nerve," was very lengthy, and embraced nearly all the school in its cast of characters. "The names of the 'stars' and their parts," says Mr. Conant, "would be interesting reading. The two 'Billy' Bateses, the Torreys, Wilder, Holmes, Waterman, Barstow, Garratt, Woods, Stetson, Hatch, Josselyn, Ramsdell, Eells, Salmond, Nash, Magoun, Wright, figured conspicuously, if my memory serves me." The singing of the quartette, Mr. Conant, B. B. Torrey, Eliza Ann Josselyn, and Elizabeth B. Sylvester, is spoken of even to this day as being remarkably fine.*

The above-mention of the Barstows reminds me of a brief poetical composition which Albert Barstow, one of our brightest boys but early called from earth, got off on one occasion —

"Composition writing is very tough.
I have written two lines and that's enough."

*Miss Sylvester subsequently married Mr. Israel H. Macomber, of Marshfield, and Miss Josselyn became the wife of Judge John H. Boult, an Amherst graduate, and now resides in Oakland, Cal.

But Mr. Conant, as I have heard, took a different view of the matter.

The Records state that on Aug. 2, 1855, Mr. Conant, who was suffering from an attack of sickness, was given leave to close the present term at the expiration of nine weeks by refunding the due proportion to scholars that have paid for the full term. Mr. C., on deciding to leave Hanover, procured a teacher without the knowledge of the Trustees, for the last two weeks of the term, whereupon they "deemed it advisable that the term close at that time."

On leaving Hanover he took charge of a new Academy in central Ohio, where he speedily recovered from his Hanover pleurisy. He afterwards taught in Kenosha, Wis., in Aurora, N. Y., in Coshocton, O., in Genesee County, N. Y., and in Plainfield, O. In many places he also served as Superintendent of Schools. His term of teaching service began in 1843 and ended in 1892. Since the latter date he has been largely engaged in pedestrianism, canyon visiting, mountain climbing, etc., and now feels himself "to be 70 years young." His present residence is Pasadena, Cal. His wife died very suddenly of heart disease in New York State in 1883. For 29 years she had been his most efficient helper in schools.

Under Mr. Conant's administration was issued the first Catalogue of Academy students which has come to my knowledge. The names are given alphabetically and in full, with places of residence annexed, and the sexes have separate columns. It contains many names which we have already met with, but I have thought it best to print it entire.

Melzar Cushing Bailey, Francis Bemis, William

HISTORY OF HANOVER ACADEMY. 81

Carver Bates, William Henry Bates, George Harvey Bates, Albert Barstow, Henry Briggs Barstow, Sidney Barstow, Haviland Barstow, Henry Payson Briggs, George C. Briggs, Charles B. Briggs, Leander Chamberlain, Samuel Joseph May Cushing, Roswell Dearborn Cushing, Nathaniel Cushing, Edwin Josselyn Chandler, Charles Henry Eells, Judson Ewell, Cyrus Collamore Holmes, Luther Wright Holmes, George Stephen Josselyn, Joseph Fobes Knapp, Charles Albert Kimball, George Allen Litchfield, Edwin Richard Litchfield, John Cushing Nash, Charles Blanchard Phillips, Henry Pratt, Levi Ramsdell, William Alfred Rogers, Moses Bass Smith Ebenezer Simmons, Daniel Kimball Stetson, Edward Gray Stetson, George Washington Sturtevant, L. Curtis Sylvester, Jethro Swett, Benjamin Barstow Torrey, Herbert Torrey, Robert Samuel Talbot, Henry Tirrell, Ebenezer Copeland Waterman, Henry Whitman, Peter Salmond Whitman, Joseph Eells Wilder, Nathaniel Walter Winslow, Henry Alexander Wood, William W. Weyer.

Helen Pauline Barker, Lucy Abby Barstow, Grace Foster Barstow, Mary Elizabeth Barstow, Caroline Louisa Barry, Elizabeth F. Billings, Mary Bradbury Church, Susan E. Cobb, Mary Webb Damon, Ellen Curtis Gardner, Harriet Lucy Garratt, Lavina Allen Hatch, Margaret P. Ives, Elizabeth B. Jones, Eliza Ann Josselyn, Priscilla Josselyn, Ophelia Litchfield, Martha Augusta Litchfield, Susan Maria Magoun, Eliza Smith Salmond, Marianna Stetson, Mary Tolman Stetson, Betsie Homer Stetson, Elizabeth Belcher Sylvester, Sarah Emily Sylvester, Martha Reed Sylvester, Helen M. Sylvester, Amelia Frances Stockbridge, Maria Warren Wright, Ellen Allston Wood. Of these, twelve came from Pembroke, thirteen from S. Scituate, forty-three belonged in Hanover, and the rest were from other places.

A Mr. Barrett, who does not seem to have been fortunate enough to leave even the initials of his given name behind him, was next chosen Principal. He began school Sept. 5, 1855 with only twenty scholars, and after keeping two days, asked the privilege to stand as a candidate for teacher of a high school in a distant place. The Trustees not granting his request, he somewhat abruptly took his leave. The scholars on assembling at the school one morning as usual, found themselves unexpectedly without a teacher.

It was thought best in this crisis that the breath of life should, if possible, be continued in the school, and so an individual from So. Scituate was urged to make the effort. Fortunately for the institution, after a few days of that gentleman's imperfect service, Mr. F. O. Barstow was secured as Principal, and he entered on his duties the thirteenth of September.

FREDERICK OLNEY BARSTOW, (1855-6), a native of Hanover, was born June 6, 1830, and graduated at Brown University in 1852. After supplying Mr. McLauthlin's place in the spring of 1853 he took a voyage to England and back, then to Canton, China, and subsequently to France *via* New Orleans. Afterward he took the preceptorship of the Academy as previously narrated and resigned the same in July, 1856. In 1857 and 1858 he took a course of lectures in medicine and surgery in Albany, N. Y., and in Boston. He married on June 28, 1858, an Academy girl, Mary Elizabeth Torrey, who died Jan. 12, 1897. He has three daughters living, all married, one of whom, Mrs. R. P. West, resides in Seattle, Wash. His first settlement as a physician was at Swampscott, 1858-61, then at San Andreas, Calaveras Co., Cal., where he was elected Principal of the grammar school and Superintendent of the schools of the County. Ordained as a minister of the Protestant Episcopal Church, July 22, 1866, he took charge of a church at Sonora and of St. Andrews Mission in San

FREDERICK OLNEY BARSTOW.

Francisco. In 1869 he returned to Massachusetts and had charge of Trinity Church, Weymouth, Nov., 1869, May 1870. He was then appointed missionary to La Messilla, New Mexico, and established the first mission and school of the P. E. Church in that territory. In 1876--79 he served as assistant minister in Grace Church, San Francisco, and in 1880 became rector of St. Peter's

Church. Since 1881 he has not had the charge of any Church, but calls himself a "Teacher and Practitioner of Divine Science." His present residence is Fruitvale, Cal. He was a born artist, and the "little cabin," 12 x 18 feet, where he is now living as he professes "a kind of hermit life," is well supplied, as I should judge from a picture, with artist's materials. The above portrait was taken in said cabin by himself, presumably with the aid of a string.

In a circular addressed by L. Vernon Briggs to "classes 1854—56" (Messrs. Conant and Barstow, Principals), I find the following new names. Possibly some of these names should appear elsewhere:

Abbie Briggs, Hannah E. Brooks, Charles W. Barstow, Henry H. Collamore, Eugene H. Clapp, Frank A. Clapp, Fred. W. Clapp, Robert S. Church, Edward Church, Hannah Davenport, Hannah B. Hart, Nathaniel Henshaw, John Magoun, Calvin T. Phillips, Charles F. Phillips, Morrill A. Phillips, Josiah Stoddard, George F. Stetson, Lydia Sylvester, Timothy Studley, W. W. Weyer.

CHARLES ANDREW REED (1856-'60), son of Samuel and Caroline (Nash) Reed, was born in Weymouth June 18, 1836, and was graduated from Amherst College in 1856. He began his services as Preceptor of the Academy Sept. 8, 1856, and continued them for fourteen terms until the first part of 1860, having had under his charge 143 different pupils. He studied law with Ellis Ames, Esq., of Canton, who was eminent both as a lawyer and as a historian, and was admitted to the bar in Boston, July 18, 1861. Since that time he has been a lawyer of distinction in Taunton, a mayor of that city, a member of the City Council, and of the Mass. Legislature (1881), and city solicitor since 1880. In June 27, 1871, he was married to Welthea N. Dean of Taunton, and has two children.

Mr. Reed, to use the words of one of his pupils, whom we have before quoted (G. F. S.), "was a most capable, faithful and successful teacher," and his service at the Academy seems to have been acceptable and successful to an unusual degree. It is therefore not strange that he says "no portion of my earlier years is so pleasant

CHARLES ANDREW REED.

as the years 1856-59, which I spent in Hanover."

Perhaps the most important event of his administration was the formation of the Alumni Association, with its several annual reunions and public celebrations, which were held about the time of Thanksgiving. The first call on the Alumni to hold a reunion meeting made by the Committee on behalf of the Alumni Association thus reads:

The Committee would respectfully request your presence at the approaching *literary festival*, and most cordially welcome you back to the scenes and associations of *Academy days*. The oration by J. E. Corlew, M. D., will be delivered Nov. 26, 1858, at the Episcopal Church in the afternoon of the day assigned for these exercises.

The Committee are assured that to you, as an old member of the Academy, the object of this Association — to revive the various associations of former days — to establish a bond of friendship between all those who have resorted thither for instruction — and to render this our educational institution worthy of your esteem and confidence — will meet a most hearty reception.

Most respectfully yours,

Chas. A. Reed,
L. C. Waterman,
D. B. Ford,
Samuel Tolman, Jr.,
E. Q. Sylvester,
T. B. Waterman,
Committee.

Dr. Corlew's Address, methinks, must be well-remembered by some to this day. In the course of his remarks he gave such a vivid and realistic description of some of his schoolmates, even of their characters and conduct, looks and habits, that many of them, and especially of the young ladies, were greatly nettled and began to dread what the next word might be.

But the whole of the afore-mentioned day was used for public celebration, and in the forenoon an Address was delivered in the Academy Hall before the "Philomathean Society" by William Carver Bates, Esq., a native of Hanover and an Alumnus who has ever greatly interested himself in the literary and financial interests of the Academy. The theme of his discourse was "The Outer and the Inner Life," and this, as he assures me, was the first public address of his life. Other public addresses of his must be remembered by many of our readers, especially the one delivered in 1877 on the 150th anniversary of the incorporation of the town, as also another delivered the next year at the dedication of the Soldiers' Monument.*

Such was the beginning of our public reunion celebrations, reminding us, by our going into the Church and our marching back and forth in procession, very strongly of our college commencements. The brass band, indeed, was wanting, and the scholastic cap and toga, but were not these within the limit of future possibilities?

In the following year, 1859, the Philomathean Society on the forenoon of Nov. 25th again held their meeting and listened to an address by Cyrus Collamore Holmes, Esq. He was son of Rev. Cyrus Holmes, and was also one of our patriot boys who enlisted and died in the war for the preservation of the Union.

In the afternoon of the same day the Alumni Asso-

---

* The doings of the latter occasion have been fitly chronicled in the Pamphlet of Dr. William Henry Brooks, but no proper historic record has been made of the preceding anniversary, which for the town was a very note-worthy affair. Its great procession, one and a half miles long, its great assemblage of between 4000 and 5000 people, its great oration by Gov. Long, its great dinner, and all its other great things should no longer be left unrecorded by the historian.

citi on were favored with an address delivered in the Episcopal Church by the Principal of the Academy, Charles A. Reed, A. M., who took the place of Rev. Marcus Ames who had been selected as orator of the day. And in the evening there was a social gathering of the members of the Association in the Academy Hall, a festival, as it was hoped to be, "of most happy memory."

Our Alumni Poetess, Mrs. Augusta (Briggs) Cheney of Worcester has kindly sent me the first of her many Alumni Poems, and I insert it here (accompanied with her recently taken portrait) as being perhaps the one which was delivered on this occasion.

MRS CHENEY

To dear old friends in front, and flank, and rear,
   On all, and every side, I make my bow.
A half fledged poet feels exceeding queer
   As all who've had experience will allow.
So I stand here, with mingled hope, and fear,
   Dreading the sentence you may chance bestow,
Like one, who waits the verdict of his life,
Or asks some doubtful maid, to be his wife.

Perhaps some critic, with his wondrous sight,
   With line, and square, and microscopic eye,
May weigh each line, and verse that I may write,
   And errors in my rhyme or rhythm may descry.
No matter! I'll admit their plebian parentage,

And all his irritating powers defy;
And still be calm, though no applause is shown,
And as their merits, claim their faults my own.

And while I make this very frank confession
   And own my lines are far from errors free,
'Tis only in the coupling or expression
   The writer's heart will bear close scrutiny,
And poetry not being my profession,
   More freely I dare hope your sympathy;
Remember, I'd no art to beautify,
But give you this, ere yet the ink is dry.

How many well-remembered faces meet my view,
   Where e'er I turn I meet familiar eyes,
And here tonight, though memory should be true,
   In seeing you I quite forget how fast time flies:
Scenes long forgotten, I in thought renew,
   My schoolgirl days in sweet remembrance rise,
And it seems but a day, since I with book in hand,
Made my debut upon this very stand.

No, not the same! for modern enterprise
   Has reared this building on the ancient site,
And though I own, to an impartial eye,
   This seems more goodly in its coat of white;
Yet deep within my heart, still lingering lies,
   A wish, I would not utter save to friends tonight,
That in its place I might see standing here,
The ancient building, brown, and square, and queer.

Those schoolgirl dreams so dear to many a heart
   Of wealth and pleasure, love and married state,
When each fair maid, seemed anxious first to part
   The golden clouds, which hid her future fate,
But still with maiden modesty would start
   If one perchance, not awed by frown sedate,
Foretelling sure their destined place in life,
Proclaimed each blushing *maid, as some man's wife.*

But time, and change, have wrought their work upon
    Those merry groups, and all their dreams are flown,
And youth's short days and fancies free are gone.
    And much we dreamed of then, we since have sadly known:
Some few remain to walk life's paths alone,
    We pity them far more than those who own
That they have halved their pains
And doubled joys, by matrimonial chains.

Marriage, and change, and death, have changed our youthful band
    And many cherished forms we miss within these walls,
Many loved tones, and kindly grasp of hands,
    Sad memory to our mind recalls,
And fate, refuses to unite the broken strands,
    Which Time has in our chain of life let fall;
But sadness ever mingles in our cup of joy,
And purest metals, mixed with base alloy.

Yet still though not unmindful of the sober past
    O'er what has been, why should we sit and croon?
Or retrospective views forever cast?
    Unmindful of the high, and priceless boon,
Of friends, and friendship, which long years may last,
    No! let us rather hope for happiness at future day,
Than sigh for buried hopes long passed away.

Our schoolgirl days may never more return,
    No more we dream, as once in days gone by,
Yet still within our hearts, shall ever burn
    The love enkindled by their memory,
And every heart shall be a sacred urn,
    Sealed with a tear, hidden from outward eye.
And friendship shall more sacred grow, as year by year
Our numbers weaken at this gathering here.

Just a week prior to this celebration, the Fall Exhibition of the Academy was held in the hall in the evening. This consisted largely of COLLOQUIES, one of which was the SCHOOL OF ORATORS, whose names were Schemer, Fickle, Bother'em, Lumper, O'Tire'em,

O'Whack'em, and Check, respectively represented by F. W. Clapp, C. B. Phillips, C. H. Eells, J. S. Crosby, K. Whitman, E. H. Clapp, and W. B. Young. Another was LE MELANGE, in which figured Stubbins, a Yankee, Linguist, Philosopher, Poet, Transcendentalist, Mathematician, Logician, Patriot and Elocutionist, who were also represented by Augustus Jacobs, F. W. Clapp, J. S. Crosby, J. P. Thorndike, C. H. Eells, K. Whitman, I. L. Waterman, and C. B. Phillips. A third colloquy was MAURICE, THE WOODCUTTER, and among the actors we see the new names of J. T. Corlew, W. I. Wright, A. L. Stetson, and Misses L. A. Hollis and A. M. Barker. Besides this was the PASTORAL OF THE SEASONS, in which Misses M. W. Robbins, P. N. Robbins, C. S. Gardner, L. A. Hollis, E. S. Salmond, H. D. Freeman, S. E. Sylvester, E. F. Haskins, A. C. Hatch, F. L. Howland, and H. P. Leach took part. Between or in addition to these parts were twenty ADDRESSES by the young gentlemen, many of whom we have mentioned, to which names we would add those of Elbridge E. Gardner, Emery Burgess, Morrill A. Phillips, Charles T. Whitman, Charles P. French, William F. Talbot, and George W. Mann. All these exercises, interspersed with Music, must have made a lengthened performance.

Perhaps we may here notice next year's Exhibition Programme (Nov. 20, 1860), which in character differs somewhat from the former one. For we have besides the speaking of pieces the delivery of original ORATIONS, viz., on Education by J. P. Thorndike, on Government by Kilborn Whitman, on the Formation of Meadows on North River by Eugene H. Clapp, on St. Stephen's Bell by Joseph T Corlew, and on Eloquence by John S. Crosby. Then there was one Colloquy, called the

Spinning Wheel and the Piano, also a brief Dialogue on the Hatter and the Printer, and the lengthy Historical Dialogue of Wilhelm Tell.

The programme of the Alumni Association for Nov. 30, 1860, announces that "the Exercises at the Episcopal Church commence at 2 1-2 P. M., and the address will be delivered by Rev. David B. Ford"; also that there will be a Social Gathering in the Hall in the evening, and addresses are expected from former Principals, an l various members of the Association. Others than alumni of the Academy have discoursed on similar occasions later in the Episcopal Church, — Mr. Peleg T. Keene in 1863, and still others perhaps, but its doors have not, I believe, since been opened to any other alumni orators.* Possibly the address of the aforementioned orator of the day finished up the business in that line for all time. If this be so, let us look at his production a little longer before dismissing it forever. Its theme was "Intellectual and Moral Culture in our Public Schools." It was afterwards printed, for substance, in the Boston Review, and was also published subsequently in pamphlet form. The author's contention in the discourse is that our public schools should not be destitute of moral and religious training and influence, while all theological teaching and sectarian dogmas should be discarded. In doing this, he considers and endeavors to answer three objections: First, That children should not be instructed in any religious tenets or doctrines until they shall have arrived at maturity of understanding, and for themselves shall be able to judge

---

* The Directors on Nov. 19, 1861, voted to grant the use of the Academy Hall on Friday evening, Nov. 22d, to the Hanover Academy Alumni Association.

between right and wrong; SECOND, That the schoolroom is not a fit place for religious instruction; that there is no natural connection or congruency between the teaching of religion and the teaching of mathematics, geography and grammar; that the mingling together of profane and sacred studies in school would tend to diminish one's reverence for the Bible; and that the proper place for imparting religious instruction is in the family circle, the church, and the Sabbath school. THIRD, However desirable in itself may be the union of intellectual and moral culture in our public schools, it is yet wholly impossible on account of the multiplicity of religions and religious sects in our land. We may state that the author began his address by quoting the law of 1647 for the establishing of public schools, which was enacted in order to thwart the wiles of " yt ould deluder, Satan," and "yt learning may not be buried in ye grave of our fathers." In closing his address, the author quotes from the last speech which Webster uttered in Faneuil Hall:

" We know that when we work upon materials immortal and imperishable, they will bear the impress which we place upon them through endless ages to come. If we work upon marble, it will perish. If we work upon brass, time will efface it. If we rear temples, they will crumble to dust. But if we work on men's immortal minds,— if we imbue them with high principles, with the just fear of God and of their fellowmen,— we engrave on those tablets something which no time can efface, but which will brighten and brighten to all eternity."

But we must not yet wholly lose sight of the Academy and its Preceptor, Mr. Reed. We see from the records that under his regime the heating by the furnace, probably a very small one, has been discontinued, and the old stove and fixings have been exchanged for a new air-tight stove; new seats have been placed at the sides of the hall, and repairs have been made on the fence, the well-curb, and the bucket-rope.[*] The summer term of 1859 was shortened to seven weeks on account of the teacher's sickness. Not long before his resignation he presents a map of Plymouth County for the benefit of the Academy. His resignation at the close of the Winter term calls forth the following vote, passed Jan. 24, 1860. "Voted, That in accepting the resignation of Mr. Charles A. Reed, M. A., the Board of Trustees take pleasure in assuring him of their high satisfaction in the services he has rendered as Principal of Hanover Academy for the last three and a half years, their regret in being deprived of his services as a Teacher, and their best wishes for his future success and happiness in the profession on which he proposes to enter."

From a partial list of Mr. Reed's pupils as furnished by himself, and from the pages of the Philomathean Library Book, I have gathered the following mostly new names. Probably several of the scholars named began with Mr. Barstow or even earlier, and some may have begun later than with Mr. Reed. There are no catalogues to help us decide on these matters.

Nathaniel Besse, Lysander F. Bates, Samuel N. Blake, Thomas D. Brooks, Emery Burgess, Edwin J. Bates, Alice Mead Barker, Sylvia A. Bourne, Sarah W.

---

[*] This windlass arrangement erelong gave place to a chain pump, and this in turn to a pump with handle, till finally pumps and well were wholly discarded.

Burgess, Amy Elizabeth Barstow, Charlotte E. Brackett, Laura A. Brewster, George H. Clapp, Elisha F. Coleman, Albert F. Curtis, Benjamin Curtis, Otis Cushing, John S. Crosby, Joseph T. Corlew, H. G. Crossley, Mary Collamore, Lucy H. Chamberlain, George F. Damon, G. F. Dwelley, Charles E. Dwelley, George Dana Doten, Franklin Thomas Doten, Mercy A. Doane. Lydia A. Damon, Sarah M. Damon, H. M. Dunbar, Abbie C. Donnell, Jennie B. Donnell, James J. Ford, Earle B. Ford, William A. Farrar, Charles P. French, Willis H. Freeman, Huldah D. Freeman, Louisa A. Farrar, Henry H. Gardner, Elbridge Everett Gardner, Charlotte S. Gardner, Thomas B. Holmes, John Hunt, John F. Hatch, Elizabeth A. Hollis, Esther Foster Haskins, Fidelia L. Howland, Mary P. Howland, Abbie Caroline Hatch, Mary D. A. Hatch, Aurelia Hall, Henry Herbert Josselyn, Augustus Jacobs, Helen M. Josselyn, Louisa C. Josselyn, Joanna Josselyn, Harriet P. Leach, George W. Mann, Florence Ella Mann, Julia M. Monroe, Rowena Orcutt, John Q. Pratt, George M. Reed, William A. Robbins, Florence V. Rogers. Mary W. Robbins, Phebe N. Robbins, Irene M. Rose, Abner L. Stetson, George E. Stockbridge, Joshua Adams Stetson, John Q. Stetson, Susan J. Stetson, F. A. Stockbridge, Susan R. Stetson, Elizabeth Stockbridge, Juletta Sylvester, Caroline T. Southworth, A. J. Sampson, J. P. Thorndike, Helen M. Thomas, Susan J. Turner, Mary C. Tolman, Rudolphus C. Waterman, F. T. Whiting, George Whiting, Warren Irving Wright, Irenaeus L. Waterman, Charles T. Whitman, Betsey H. Whiting, Lucinda E. Wilder, Emily Waters, William B. Young.

On the date last mentioned, SAMUEL G. STONE (1860--

61), a graduate of Amherst in 1859, was chosen Principal to commence his services with the Spring term, Feb. 27, 1860. He was son of Thomas S. and Martha (Spaulding) Stone, and was born in Cavendish, Vt., Oct. 30, 1833. After leaving Hanover he taught in Rochester, Ware, Westerly, R. I., and Charlestown, and is now an insurance broker and florist in the last-named place.

In Aug. 6, 1866, he married Alice P., daughter of Elijah Beaumont of East Hartford, Ct., but, I think, has no children.

Mr. Stone was a thorough classical and general scholar,* and brought the highest recommendations from his teachers; but owing to an imperious or impetuous disposition, he and the official powers soon came into collision. On Dec. 17 a meeting was called to confer with Mr. Stone as to some complaints respecting the government of the school and objectionable language used by him towards the pupils, — the purpose of the meeting being to advise Mr. S. in some things in which the Trustees thought him indiscreet. More definite action was taken on Feb. 8, 1861, when a committee was appointed "to state to him the dissatisfaction of the Trustees and parents with his want of self-control in the government of the school, and the opinion of the Trustees that on the whole it is best for the interests of the school to make a change of Instructors." At a meeting of Feb. 11 this Committee reported that Mr. Stone was not ready to say whether he would resign at the close of the term, or take, as per agreement, three

---

*It is related as one of his attainments that he never could be "spelled down." At a spelling match in Music Hall he won a $600 Steinway piano.

months' notice. At the same meeting a Committee was chosen to make inquiries for a new Principal. Shortly after this, Mr. Stone gave out notice that he would continue three months. On March 11, a meeting of the Proprietors was called to act on the petition of Seth Barker and others that the services of Mr. Stone be retained. This meeting was largely attended by spectators, — Mr. S. having requested his scholars to come and to invite their friends; but the time of the meeting was largely taken up in discussing the fourth article of the Constitution touching the power of the Trustees to dismiss a Teacher. Finally after long debate it was voted to dissolve the meeting and consequently the petition was not acted upon. The next day after this meeting Mr. Stone made known his determination to remain in the school and to contest his right by purchasing a share of the stock if necessary. Whereupon another meeting of the Proprietors was held April 8, to act upon the matter of the continuance or non-continuance of Mr. Stone's services, when it was " Resolved " by a stock vote of the Proprietors, 47 voting affirmatively and none in the negative, " that the services of Mr. Samuel G. Stone end at the close of the present term, Tuesday, May 14, 1861, provided the Trustees concur in said vote." On this closing day of the school, thirty two scholars were present; and all the Trustees were in attendance, and at the close of the exercises the Secretary, Capt. Elijah Barstow, read to the school the following notices:

1st. The Trustees give notice that by vote of the Proprietors and the concurrence of the Trustees of Hanover Academy, the services of Mr. Stone as Principal of the Academy end this day.

2d. The Trustees in behalf of the Proprietors and themselves would inform Mr. Stone and all who are interested that he can no longer occupy these premises, and we hereby notify him to remove forthwith his books and effects from the building.

3d. The Trustees also give notice that they have unanimously elected Mr. P. T. Keene, Jr., in place of Mr. Stone, who will commence the summer term on Monday next, May 20th, 1861.

From what the Trustees know of Mr. Keene they confidently recommend him to all who are interested in the welfare of their children, as competent for the position to which they have chosen him." *

The next page of the records has this statement: "Saturday night, May 18, 1861. A mob led by Samuel G. Stone assisted by John S. Crosby, assistant teacher, broke into the Academy by battering the door and gained possession of the building." We may remark that the building had been garrisoned after Mr. Stone had been once ejected therefrom, but the guards could not resist this modern Cæsar and his forces, armed with stones, brickbats and battering-ram. Among Mr. Stone's abettors in this work of darkness were not only his personal friends and sympathizers, not only a big crowd of the commonalty, men and boys, urging on the contest with their shouts and cheers, but even some of the youthful soldiers, who were making the old Academy their rendezvous while preparing for the civil war, enlisted in Mr. Stone's behalf and did valiant home-service on this occasion ere they shed their blood on the Southern battlefields. And thus was this our Sumter

---

* Mr. Keene had previously taught in our Public Schools.

taken (not long after the Southern Sumter) and held by the besiegers with force and arms ; and Mr. Stone began his school in the Academy building, May 20, 1861.

Early in June an Appeal was made to the Supreme Court by Mr. Stone's lawyer, Hon. Perez Simmons, * for an injunction to keep the Trustees from interfering with his School, on the ground that he was an owner in common of the property, but Judge Hoar decided that Mr. Stone had thereby no exclusive rights to the premises. The Trustees, however, compromised the matter and granted Mr. S. possession on certain conditions until the close of the Summer term. On leaving the school he gave to the Trustees a deed of his share, but he failed in his promise to leave the building in good condition, and the Trustees found some of the apparatus missing or injured.

The records also state that Mr. P. T. Keene, Jr., of Duxbury, the newly elected Principal of Hanover Academy, began the summer term also on May 20, 1861, in the Lecture Room of the Episcopal Church, but on account of sickness he left the next day and was not able to recommence until June 19. Length of term seven weeks, number of scholars sixteen. Both of the schools closed at the same time, Aug. 2, 1861.

At the next meeting of the Board, June 19, it was resolved to incorporate the Academy under Chapter 67 of the General Laws of Massachusetts.

The incorporation was effected August 14, 1861, under the auspices of Benjamin W. Harris of East Bridgewater, Justice of the Peace, afterwards a mem-

---

* Mr. Simmons, born in Hanover in 1811, and a graduate from Brown University in 1833, was for a short time a student in the Academy, probably when under the Preceptorship of Mr. Bates.

ber of Congress, and a Judge of Probate for Plymouth County. The casting of votes was as follows: Total in the affirmative, for incorporation, twenty-nine votes, representing eighty-two shares. Total in the negative, two votes, representing three shares. Total absent or not voting, thirteen persons representing twenty shares.

After this vote, Lemuel C. Waterman was by ballot elected Clerk of the Corporation, who was then called forward and sworn to the faithful performance of all his duties as Clerk of the Corporation of Hanover Academy by the presiding Justice who then vacated the chair.

Thankful we are that the war is over and that no blood has been shed; but there are some results of the "late unpleasantness" which we must notice. The field, indeed, was dispossessed of the belligerents, but they, encouraged by Perez Simmons and others, set up a school some three or four miles distant, in "Snappet," which was naturally regarded as an opposition movement. Mr. Stone, however did not continue his administration in this "Assinippi Institute" more than two or three years, nor did it, as subsequently conducted by Mr. Crosby and others a few years longer, much injure the Academy. Then there were home damages and expenses to pay for. Our fort needed repairing, and the bill for repairs was $31.20. There were also counsel fees—a bill of Messrs. Harris and Jewell for $50, and of Charles F. Choate, Esq. the long time President of the Old Colony Rail Road, for $40.25, expenses of keepers (guards of the building) $35.40, witnesses to Boston, $8.50. To pay these and other items, Mrs. Eliza Salmond gave $50, George Curtis $25, John Cushing $20, E. Q. Sylvester and Dr. Freeman Foster $15 each, Rev. Samuel Cutler and Isaac

H. Haskins $10 each, Dr. Joseph B. Fobes, Rev. Joseph Freeman, Elijah Barstow and T. H. C. Barstow $5 each, Nathaniel Barstow, $3, and Dr. John O. French $2. Received also $3.93 from sale of Mr. Stone's share. And thus the whole bill of expense for law-suit and damages, amounting to nearly $200, was paid.

Mr. Stone continued to reside in Hanover, as we have seen, for some time longer. For two or three years he served as member of the School Committee, and as Secretary of that Committee he wrote for the year 1862-3 a long and able School Report, covering twenty-four printed pages.

JOHN S. CROSBY.

Mr. JOHN S. CROSBY, of whom mention has been made, is a descendant of Simon Crosby, an early emigrant to the Massachusetts Colony, and was born in Waldo County, Maine, Jan. 13, 1842. In early life he came to Massachusetts, studied in our Academy and taught therein and in many of our schools, and was regarded as one of the most inspiriting and successful of our teachers. I personally knew of his ability as a teacher and disciplinarian in some of the district schools of So. Scituate when I was a member of the school committee in that town. In 1866 he was called West to take charge of the High School at St. Joseph, Mo., and was a most successful master of that school for some twelve years. After this he was settled as a lawyer for about ten years in Kansas City, Mo. About this time he began to take a special interest in industrial and social questions, and at length became a "populist" agitator and leader. As a platform speaker he stands in the opinion of many, almost unrivalled for magnetic and effective oratory, and has been called "the Wendell Phillips of the single tax movement." In 1896 he published a work entitled: "An Inquiry into the Nature and Functions of a State." In 1897 he removed to New York, and has now a law office in that city. He was twice married and has one daughter living near us, Mrs. Louise C. Drew of West Roxbury.

The Academy having now been incorporated with the desire and design that no *emeute* like the one above described should ever happen again, the Directors at a meeting held Aug. 26, 1861 voted that Rev. Messrs Cutler and Freeman be a Committee to confer with Mr. Peleg T. Keene, Jr. the present Principal of the Academy, in relation to the adoption of such rules and regulations as they may deem expedient for the protection of the Academy buildings, grounds, and fences from injury, also in relation to the deportment of the pupils. Whereupon on Sept. 2, they issued the following rather stringent rules for the proper regulation and government of the school.

1. There shall be no rough playing in the building, such as throwing balls, standing upon or running over the desks and seats; no injury shall be done to the fence, trees, or any other property; no pencil or other marks on the wall.

2. Any scholar injuring the building, its furniture, or the trees, fence or anything pertaining to the Academy shall be held responsible for the damage he may commit. When the person or persons are unknown there shall be charged for the damage, pro rata, in all the bills as " Damage to Property."

3. No scholar shall leave the premises at recess without permission from the Principal.

4. No scholar is allowed to enter or leave the Academy building except by the door.

5. No scholar shall go into the Attic or Belfry except the Bell-ringer, and he only when it is necessary to arrange the bell or other things pertaining to the building.

6. No scholar is allowed to throw any paper or other article upon the floor.

7. There shall be no profane swearing, no indecorous language.

8. There shall be no use of tobacco in any form on the premises.

9. Any scholar persisting in violating either of these rules shall be expelled from the school.

10. (Additional). No guns or other fire-arms are allowed on the premises.

Possibly from the adoption of these rules at this time our readers may draw an inference, rightly or wrongly, as to the Academic history of the recent past.

With the name of Mr. PELEG T. KEENE (1861-64) we have already become somewhat familiar He was the son of Peleg T. and Ruth Keene, and was born in Marshfield Oct. 21, 1841. We have already spoken of his first term in Hanover. In his Second or Fall term he had thirty-five scholars. His programme for the Spring term, Feb. 24, 1862, announces Edward Southworth as Assistant, and Susan A. Smith of N. Pembroke as teacher of music. Mr. Keene, it will be recollected, began to teach here in troublous times with only a handful of scholars, yet his last three terms had an average attendance of nearly forty-seven.

On leaving here at the end of the Spring term, 1864,

PELEG T. KEENE.

the Directors on April 26 passed the following Resolve: "That in accepting the resignation of Mr. Peleg T. Keene, Jr. who for three years has so satisfactorily filled the office of Principal of Hanover Academy, we would tender to him our appreciation of his untiring efforts in promoting the welfare of the pupils under his care, and that we congratulate him in view of his very popular and successful term of service. The Directors would assure him of their interest in his future welfare, and their hope that he may be as useful and prosperous in the profession or calling upon which he may enter, as he has been as a teacher among us."

After leaving Hanover, Mr. Keene went to North Adams as assistant engineer on the tunnel, and was shortly after called to Washington as clerk in the Bureau of Yards and Docks, and while residing there he studied medicine in the Georgetown College and graduated at the head of his class. Subsequently, Dr. Keene was appointed Health Officer of Washington, which office he held for a number of years. For a long time he was there associated with Dr. D. W. Bliss of "Condurango" medicine fame. He married in 1875 Miss A. Fannie Reed of Rockland, who died of consumption in 1878, leaving one son. After this he went to Portland, Oregon. His death occurred in Mansfield, Mass., while on a visit to his sister, Mrs. George C. Soule who now lives in Boston. "At the time of his death in 1889 he was connected with a chain of hospitals from the Atlantic to the Pacific coast."

I think the following were mostly new scholars under Mr. Keene or at about his time.

Marcus F. Ames, Jerome K. Briggs, George Briggs, Frank Baker, George Baker, James E. Bates, Edward G. Barnard, George W. Barnard, Etta H. Barstow, Delia L. Baker, Alice M. Barker, Josiah A. Chandler, Henry Currell, Benjamin Church, Walter R. Clift, James C. Church, Ida M. Chamberlain, Bertie H. Cobb, Reuben C. Donnell, E. Frances Damon, Vesta Ewell, Mary L. Eells, Charles A. Foster, C. T. French, Henry B. Holmes, Israel Hatch, Edward Haskins, Rebecca J.

Joyce, Wesley W. Kender, James Kent, George W. Lewis, Sarah F. Merritt, Urban Percival, Grace H. Phillips, Annie M Polden, Isabella J. Pratt, Charles F. Randall, Carrie E. Randall, William Henry Savage, Horace M. Stetson, Edward Shepherd, William Stephens, Edward Southworth, Sidney Soule, Melvin W. Stetson, Lorenzo S. Sherman, Herman Sturtevant, John F. Savage, Emma L. Stoddard, Emma B. Stockbridge, Waldo Tilden, Charles P. Turner, Horace S. Tower, Herbert A. Thorndike, Frank A. Tower, Fred Tower, Wendell P. Thayer, Mary B. Turner, Addie W. Turner, Fannie J. Wright, Jennie Widdows, Katie Wood.

EDWARD SOUTHWORTH.

EDWARD SOUTHWORTH, for a time Mr. Keene's assistant in mathematics while a pupil in the Academy, was son of James and Julia (Tilden) Southworth, and was born in So. Scituate, April 26, 1838. After honorable service in the Civil War he was elected Representative to the Legislature from the third district Plymouth Co. in the Fall of 1865. Appointed Principal of the Coddington Grammar School, Quincy, in 1866; teacher in the Dwight School, Boston, Sept. 1867, sub-master in the Rice School, Sept. 1869, and in 1878 was appointed master of the Mather School, which position he now holds. In Dec. 2, 1859 he was married to an Academy pupil, Eliza S. Talbot who died May 16, 1864, while he was in the army, leaving one daughter, Fannie Baldwin, born Feb. 20, 1861. He was married again to Hattie E. Hill of Sherborn, May, 1, 1867, and has two children living, E. Frank and Stacy B. Southworth.

Mr. Keene's Music Teacher, Miss SUSAN A. SMITH, of North Pembroke, has in late years given herself more especially to historical and genealogical research, —being, as she describes herself "a busy woman with the ancestral trees."

Under Mr. Keene's administration, and in the midst of our great Civil War an Exhibition was held in the Academy Hall Friday evening, May 3, 1863. The following is a full programme of the exercises. Our readers will perceive that it savors largely of the war-spirit.

MUSIC.—All together once again.
DECLAMATIONS.—
    Latin Extract: Speech of Adherbal to the Roman Senate.
                                              Willis H. Freeman
    God bless our Stars   .   .   .   .   S. B. Thorndike
DIALOGUE.—Not an Uncommon Complaint.
    John Doe   . . .   . . Charles F. Randall
    Richard Roe   .   .   Charles A. Foster
READING.—What is Life.   . Lizzie E. Stockbridge
COLLOQUY.—Dogmatism.
    Upper Dog   James C. Church
    Under Dog   . Herbert A. Thorndike
    Outside Dog   .   Reuben C. Donnell
MUSIC.—The Echo.
TABLEAU.— The Bridal Prayer .   Miss L. E. Stockbridge
DECLAMATIONS.—
    Early Rising   . .   . Emery Burgess
    Peace to the West   Edward G. Barnard

The Sword of Bunker Hill — Daniel H. Welch
DRAMA.—Counterplot
  Mrs Vilmont (a widow of decayed fortune) — Susie A. Smith
  Sophia (her daughter) — Lizzie S. Salmond
  Allan } her sons — Joseph T. Corlew
  Henry } — Charles T. Whitman
  The Magistrate — George W. Barnard
  Eveline (an orphan heiress) — Lizzie E. Stockbridge
  Matilda (her friend) — Annie E. Eells
  Viola (a servant).
DECLAMATIONS.—
  Upward! Onward! — H. A. Thorndike
  Our Country — Edward Haskins
TABLEAU.—Day and Night — { Abbie C. Donnell / Emma B. Stockbridge }
READING. Revolutionary Story — Lizzie S. Salmond
MUSIC. There's a Sigh in the Heart.
DIALOGUE. Discretion the Better Part of Valor.
  General Feathers — J. T. Corlew
  Corporal Blunt — E. G. Barnard
  Captain Wary — Emery Burgess
  Private Gore — Charles T. Whitman
DECLAMATION. Words for the Hour — Edward Ring
MUSIC. Welcome to May.
DIALOGUE. Juvenile Rebellion.
  Blushrose — Etta H. Barstow
  Mintdrop — Annie E. Eells
  Silvertop — Mary L. Eells
  Amaranth — Amy E. Barstow
  Cantelope — Jennie Widdows
  Major Spindle — Charles F. Randall
  General Slasher — S. B. Thorndike
  Orator Splurge — Charles A. Foster
  Citizen Toppie — Reuben C. Donnell
  Sergeant Muddle — Edward Ring
  Corporal Tipkins — H. A. Thorndike
DECLAMATIONS.
  Crowning Glory — Emery Burgess
  The Polish Boy — Joseph T. Corlew
MUSIC. Battle Cry of Freedom.

Mr. Keene's term of service in Hanover was distinguished by gifts made to the Academy fund by JOHN BARSTOW, ESQ., of Providence. The following is a copy of the letter in which he makes his principal donation.

To the Trustees and Proprietors of Hanover Academy.

GENTLEMEN.—Having a desire to aid in supporting a good school in my native village, I have for that purpose deposited with my much esteemed and trustworthy

JOHN BARSTOW.

friend Benjamin B. Torrey, a U. S. Treasury Note, of One Thousand Dollars, bearing interest from the 19th of February last at the rate of 7 3-10 per cent. per annum.

This one thousand dollars, I present to the Trustees and Proprietors of the Hanover Academy recently incorporated, and their successors, in Trust, as and for a "Permanent Fund," the income derived therefrom is to be applied to the support of the Academy in the following manner.

First.—Keeping the Buildings in good repair.

Second.—Furnishing the School from time to time with Maps, Atlases, Books of Reference, and with such School apparatus as may be necessary for illustrating the Branches that may be taught,—meaning thereby such as are not usually furnished by Teachers or Scholars.

For Trustees of this "Permanent Fund" I hereby appoint the Treasurer of the Corporation, ex officio, and his successor, and the above named Benjamin B. Torrey—authorizing them to invest said Fund from time to time in any safe and productive property or securities, and to change said investment at their discretion, —and I also authorize the Trustees of the Corporation to appoint a Trustee to the "Permanent Fund" to supply the place of said Benjamin B. Torrey whenever it shall become vacant by his resignation or death.

Providence April 18/62
John Barstow.

At a meeting held April 28, 1862, the Directors in view of Mr. Barstow's generous gift passed the following :

"Resolved: That the Board of Directors in behalf of themselves and the Corporation, express to Mr. Barstow their grateful sense of obligation for the judicious and timely gift of one thousand dollars which he has given to aid in supporting a good school in his native village.'"

This fund is now deposited in the Warren Institution for Savings, Charlestown, Mass.*

In January, 1863, Mr. Barstow made a proposition to the Trustees for the erection of an out-building for the female department after his own pattern and at his own expense. This building as subsequently erected under the supervision of Lemuel Cushing Waterman, Esq., must have cost, I suppose, towards two hundred dollars.

One other donation to the Academy in 1863, was that of a piano which the Preceptor hitherto had hired at an annual rent of thirty-two dollars. It was offered for one hundred dollars in cash, and towards its purchase Samuel Cutler and George Curtis gave twenty dollars each, Mrs. Salmond fifteen dollars, Peleg T. Keene twelve dollars, John Cushing ten dollars, and others gave smaller sums.

ARTHUR SEWELL LAKE (1864-65), son of David and Julia B. (Sanborn) Lake, was born in Chicester, N. H., Nov. 11, 1837, graduated at Dartmouth 1862, became Principal of Conway Academy, Mass. in 1862, of Hingham Academy in 1863, and of Hanover Academy, May 16, 1864. Prior to his coming here it would seem that

---

*I have a letter in my possession, dated Providence, Dec. 28, 1897, from Mr. John Barstow's two daughters, expressing their desire that, in case the Academy should be permanently closed, the fund should be devoted to the Hanover Free Library. They express themselves as being " sure that their father would wish it."

Furthermore in carrying out their desire, they on Dec. 19, 1898, signed a legal document authorizing the Trustees of said Barstow fund to pay it over to the Trustees of the Hanover Free Library, the income of which is to be used for the purchase of books in general accord with the instrument of trust as made to the Academy.

he taught in Titicut, North Middleboro, Academy, for its trustees "recommend him as a worthy young man and an accomplished and efficient teacher." My neighbor, Dr. Clarence L. Howes who was fitted for college under Mr. Lake calls him "a fine classical scholar and a good teacher." His letters of application date from

ARTHUR SEWELL LAKE

Loudon, N. H. Having received a louder call he resigned at Hanover April 1865, and went to Thomaston, Ct. where he taught several years in the Academy which was erected for his use at a cost of $12,000, which was collected by himself. Subsequently he taught in West Winsted and in Torrington, Ct., and in 1873 went to Shenandoah, Iowa, his present residence, and has from that time been engaged in the real estate business. In Thomaston, he married one of his pupils, and has one daughter who is a teacher, and a son who is connected with a bank in that place. In politics, he declares himself to be "a sound money Republican, and in religion, still a Congregationalist."

In his Hanover reminiscences he speaks of the wonderful performance of the school in gymnastics, of which he in practice knew nothing.* He says: "I can still see them, in mind, marching, counter-marching, circling, and turning hither and thither, almost getting into knots, but finally all evolved free from blunder or failure in the least. The ladies had a special costume for the exercise." As his teaching here was in war times he one day arranged to have the school sing "John Brown's body." One of the pupils, now a staid Aesculapius in our village, expecting a solemn, grave and slow song, was so struck with the novelty of the speed and apparent hilarity of the tune, that, as soon as they commenced singing, he began to laugh, and kept it up till the song was ended. One day there was a ship-launching, and "we all went down to the ship yard to see the launching, the first and last sight of that kind to me." While visiting the home of Daniel Webster in Marshfield (April 15, 1865), the church bell there began to toll for the death of Abraham Lincoln on the day previous. He brought the news back to Hanover, and "we tolled the two church bells in honor of the dead."

The Summer term following Mr. Lake's resignation seems to have been omitted.

---

* I find from the Records that the Academy Treasurer at about this time received $8.25 from a "gymnastic class" for the use of the Hall.

During his stay in Hanover, some $50, of the Barstow Fund was expended for the purchase of reference books. We may also add here that in the Summer of 1866 Mr. Isaac M. Wilder presented to the Academy a large collection mainly of College and Classical books which doubtless belonged to his son, Joseph E. Wilder who left his studies in Amherst College to enlist in the war, and was killed in battle.

ISAIAH DOLE (1865), son of Wigglesworth and Elizabeth (Haskell) Dole, was born in Bloomfield, now Skowhegan, Me., May 23, 1819. After graduating from Bowdoin College in 1840 he gave himself to the work of instruction, making a specialty of Latin and Greek. He taught at Bluehill Academy, 1843-47, in St. Stephens Academy, N. B., in Gorham Seminary, though not continuously, 1848-64, and at Lasell Seminary, Auburndale, 1875-81. He was chosen as Preceptor of our Academy out of seven applicants who had visited Hanover (there were fifteen applications in all), and he began here Sept. 4, 1865, and resigned in November, after teaching but one term. He was doubtless discouraged by the smallness of the school, though he had twenty-seven scholars. After leaving Auburndale he resided in Keene, N. H. where he died May 17, 1892 of pulmonary consumption. In Aug. 18, 1844 he married Elizabeth T. Pearson who died in 1851, leaving two children, one of whom, Edmund P. Dole, now of Seattle, Wash., attended the Academy. A daughter, Mrs. William J. Sewall, resides in Keene, N. H. Mr. Dole was a frequent contributor to educational and religious periodicals, and during the closing years of his life spent much time upon a comparative grammar of the

English and Latin languages, which however he left incomplete. He was undoubtedly one of the best scholars that ever taught in our school. The Academy Trustees, in their printed notice, justly say that "Mr. Dole comes highly recommended as a gentleman of great experience in teaching, and of high literary attainments."

JOHN P. APTHORP (1865–66) son of a Congregational minister, was born in Quincy, Ill., Sept. 7, 1839. After residing for brief periods in different places in the West he came to N. Bridgewater, now Brockton, in 1854, and was fitted for college in the Academy of that place under the tuition of Mr. S. D. Hunt. After graduating from Amherst in 1861, he taught for a brief space in Conway Academy (1861–2) and in Myricksville near Taunton. "Overcome by a wave of patriotism" in 1862, he enlisted for the war in the 10th Mass. Battery Light Artillery which joined the Army of the Potomac just after the battle of Gettysburg, and which took part in all the battles and campaigns of that army until the surrender at Appomatox. Of his two brothers who entered the army one was killed in battle near Decatur, Ala. in 1864. Returning North he soon after became Principal of Hanover Academy and taught the Winter term of 1865–6. "My relations," he says, "with the pupils and people of Hanover Four Corners were very pleasant, in some respects more so than in any other place where I ever taught. My recollections of a sleigh ride which the school took that Winter are still very fresh. At the close of the term the pupils presented me with a Bible which I keep as a valued souvenir of that time." Following a brother to Florida he engaged somewhat unsuccessfully in orange growing, also quite largely in government surveying and in teaching, and was for a time Superintendent of Schools in Leon County. On removing to Tallahassee he bought a small property near by, and has since devoted his time chiefly to his dairy-farm. In 1892 he was attacked by a nervous disease which has disabled him ever since. His letter to me had to be written by another hand.

In August, 1873, he visited Massachusetts, and was married at Ipswich to Miss Ellen Osgood of Fryeburg, Me., who died in her Florida home April 23, 1896, leaving three daughters, the eldest of whom, Mary, graduated two years ago at the head of her class in the West Florida Seminary.

In March, 1866, MR. PETER L. WOODBURY[*] was engaged as teacher to take the place of George Henry Bliss, of Vermont, who was accepted to begin Feb. 26, but who failed to meet his engagement. Mr. Woodbury, the son of Jesse and Hannah (Duncklee) Woodbury, was born in Francestown, N. H., May 4, 1840, graduated at Dartmouth, 1865, began teaching here March 12, 1866, and closed the school with a shortened term, July 12, 1867, to take the High School in Foxboro. Though his school closed with only seventeen scholars, yet the Records say that during most of the year the school was "in a satisfactory condition." In his vacation, Aug., 1866, he writes from Francestown on the expediency of advertising the Academy. He states that he has had an offer of a High School, but hopes he would do as well by

---

[*] This is his name as found in his letters, though the Academy Records give S. as his middle initial; and yet in all his college course he is registered without any middle name. The L... as I am told, stands for Levi.

remaining in Hanover, and he fears that his good friends here would be disconcerted by such a change.

Of his later history, I have only learned that he taught for three or four years in the Holderness School at Plymouth, N. H., and that he left P. in 1892 to teach a High School in Eastport, Me.

For some years past we have had no list of students, but I think that those whose names here follow newly entered either under Mr. Woodbury, or his predecessors, Apthorp, Dole, or Lake.

Henry S. Bartlett, Walter S. Barker, J. Williams Beal, Alice Briggs, Lizzie Barrows, George Currell, Frank Clapp, H. E. Chamberlain, Frank Collamore, Susie W. Clift, Delia F. Carey, Rose Corbett, Nellie Clapp, Clara M. Chase, Clara Crooker, Florence R. Cushing, Belle Cushing, Rosie M. Cobbin, Sarah C. Church, E. P. Dole, Nancy C. Donnell, Annie E. Eells, Abbie Estes, Avis Ford, Agnes H. Freeman, Justus Gardner, Briggs Gulliver, Clarence L. Howes, Jennie B. Hersey, Susan P. Hatch, Beulah S. Holmes, Charles Josselyn, Isaac Keene, Abbie Kilbrith, Maria Leonard, John J. McFarland, Herbert E. Reed, Frank A. Reed, Coolidge Roberts, Sarah A. Russell, Irene Rose, Edwin Stockbridge, Alice R. Shepherd, Carrie Stearns, Martha E. Snell, Eunice P. Simmons, Mary Savage, Ella B. Stetson, Roger Tappan, Ella J. Thomas, Frank H. Waterman, Herbert Witherell, Amey Young.

EBENEZER BRADFORD GAY, of Dighton, was next chosen Principal. He began the school with 24 pupils, Sept. 2, 1867, and resigned the following November, having only 16 paying scholars. Verily, if it can be said that the Academy was alive during this recent period, it was living, apparently, at a poor dying rate.

John Prince Thorndyke, (1867—68, with Mary L. Eells for assistant), "was born in Boston, Jan. 16, 1846. In May, 1852 he was taken to Samuel Brown's in Pembroke, where he attended boarding school for boys, held on the premises. His tutors in this school were Messrs. Storrs, Willard, Crehore and George R. Dwelley, of Hanover, the latter being one of the most famous teachers in Massachusetts. Here he remained as long as the school continued, or until the spring of 1856. In June, 1856, he began attendance at the Academy, and continued as a pupil until Dec. 18, 1862, making an attendance of 26 *consecutive* terms with only an absence of *five* days. His teachers in the Academy were Messrs. F. O. Barstow, C. A. Reed, S. G. Stone, and P. T. Keene.

"Besides enjoying the advantage of a longer term of instruction in this institution than any other pupil, it may be of interest to note that with the exception of Mr. F. O. Barstow [and Charles Hitchcock] the subject of this sketch is the only person who ever was both pupil and preceptor of the Academy. On December 8, 1867, he began his labors as principal of the school which was in a very weak condition, numbering only 16 pupils; but by unfaltering perseverance he soon raised the reputation of the school to its old time status, and when he closed his work, Nov. 20, 1868, he had the satisfaction of knowing he had made a successful effort as results in all directions abundantly proved. In the spring of 1860 he became interested in religion, and was christened into the Episcopal Church, Hanover, by Rev. Samuel Cutler, July 15, and was confirmed by Bishop Eastburn June 25, 1861. In March 8, 1869, he was baptized in Niagara river at Tonawanda, N. Y., and united with the

"Disciples of Christ" denomination, in many places known as the "Christian" denomination.

"On Aug. 30, 1869, he was married to Flora J. Straight, in Rochester, N. Y., by whom he had four boys. June 20, 1894, he was married to Agnes W. Gleason, of Plymouth, Mass. Upon the transition of his little three-year old boy, in 1879, totally failing to find a particle of consolation (for which he so yearned) in his religion, his Bible or his church, he gave them all up as broken, unreliable reeds. After mature deliberation and most thorough investigation into the claims of Spiritualism he became convinced of the truth of its philosophy, and associated himself with that sect. He has been for 13 years an earnest public worker on the platform, and during that time has labored in 13 different States. In 1894 he was duly ordained as a minister of the gospel of Spiritualism."

The reader will observe that in the above sketch I have used quotation marks, because the writer, unlike any other of my correspondents, *sincerely* hopes I "will not leave out a word." I do not know whether this request was prohibitory of my adding a word or not. Had I taken my usual liberty I could have spoken of some interesting matters which Mr. Thorndyke has omitted. I will simply add that the Academy authorities would have retained him longer, but he hoped for something better in the great West. The Academy was closed one term after his leaving. He states in a letter recently received that "After leaving the Academy he was called to take charge of the public schools of Tonawanda, N. Y., and that he has been engaged in the commercial world, East, West and South." His present residence is Flint, Michigan, where he has recently established a small monthly paper, called THE FLINT MESSENGER, "an exponent of liberal thought." I expected to present his likeness, but for some unknown reason I have failed to hear from him of late.

We are happy to present here a full and accurate list of Students under Mr. Thorndike which he himself furnished for this work. We print it in full and as he wrote it, though it contains a few names already mentioned.

Henry S. Bartlett, William Briggs, William P. Brooks, Samuel J. May Brooks, Charles E. Collamore, Edwin A. Collamore, Frank B. Collamore, Francis Collamore, George N. Curtis, Abner L. Curtis, Seth A. Curtis, Patrick Christy, Reuben C. Donnell, Manley J. Gurney, William J. Hodge, Willard T. Hatch, Gilman S. Josselyn, J. Austin Knapp, Samuel S. Knapp, Thomas Loring, James Murphy, Charles B. Muich, Herbert W. Otis, E. Frank Otis, Horace D. Osgood, Frank A. Reed, Lorenzo S. Sherman, Daniel A. Sherman, Fred C. Stetson, Samuel Tolman 3d, Richmond Talbot, Frank H. Torrey, Miles S. Turner, Charles P. Turner, Frank H. Waterman, Edwin C. White, William B. Wood.

Fannie H. Barstow, Clara M. Chase, Lizzie O. Cushing, Annie Church, M. Jennie Currell, Alice H. Curtis, Nancie C. Donnell, Nellie H. Ford, Sarah J. Flavell, Mary E. Flavell, M. Ella Farrar, Ida H. Frinsdorff, Mary L. Foster, Lucy J. Gurney, Fannie A. Hobill, Lizzie M. Howard, Welthea M. Magoun, Katie McCurdy, Annie A. Murphy, Mary A. Oldham, Sarah A. Russell, Alice R. Shepherd, Mary E. Sturtevant, Addie M. Stockbridge, Lucy P. Stockbridge, Ruthena Stockbridge, Louisa O. Stetson, Lucy A. Stetson, Ann E. Stetson, E. Ellen Savage, Sarah E. Studley, Julia E. .

Sylvester, Grace Thorndike, Mary P. Tower, Mary S. Turner, Emma H. Torrey, Ella J. Thomas.

JOSEPHINE McRoy (1869-70), of Saxonville, was born in Framingham Jan. 28, 1850 and was graduated from the Saxonville High School in 1865 and from the Framingham Normal School in Jan. 1869, and is now the wife of Mr. Israel Hatch, an Alumnus of the

JOSEPHINE McROY.

Academy, and for some time past a member of the School Committee of Norwell. She, as sole Principal, began teaching in the Academy March 1, 1869, for $500 per year, the first recorded instance of an Academy teacher's receiving a stated salary. In July 18, 1870, she resigned her principalship on account of ill health, the last term being shortened one half. In her first term she had twenty-three scholars and in her second term twenty-seven, and the annual Report states that she taught "satisfactorily and successfully." Dr. H. L. Sweeny who was one of her pupils, states in his Historical Address of 1889, that she "was very popular with the pupils, especially the large boys of whom there was quite a number." At the close of her administration, however, the prospects of the school were not encouraging. The Treasurer, Rev. Samuel Cutler, in his Report, Aug. 5, 1870 says: "The establishment of a High School in Hanover and also in Pembroke, while lessening the number of scholars in the Academy, is also rendering it somewhat doubtful whether and how long it can be sustained." The Academy, however, was sustained for some twenty years longer, partly by means of an Alumni fund, the raising of which took place at about this time.

In the first part of 1860, the chairman of the Alumni Committee, William Carver Bates, sent out the following notice:

"ALUMNI FUND.

All persons interested in the prosperity of Hanover Academy, are invited to contribute to an Alumni Fair to be held at Hanover some time during the next Summer in the Academy building. The particulars will be announced hereafter. This is to urge every Alumnus to begin early in the work of preparing and sending forward articles for sale at the Fair. Packages may be sent to Mrs. Edmund Q. Sylvester, Hanover, Mass., or to the subscriber at Boston.

It is proposed to give a subscription Entertainment, musical and literary, in behalf of the fund at the Academy Hall, Feb. 22, 1869, tickets to which may be had of the

Committee. Let us all contribute to the prosperity of our Alma Mater."

On the day of the Subscription entertainment a communication (signed, "S. C.") was handed to the chairman of the Alumni Committee, stating that "For the encouragement of such an effort (to raise subscriptions for the fund) . . . you may say that a friend of the Academy, and in memoriam of one who was for a little time a pupil in the old building, but now deceased, [S. Gardner Cutler, died Feb. 12, 1869], will give $100 toward the fund. It will not be necessary for you *publicly* to announce the name" etc.

From the proceeds of the fair which was held in August 1869 amounting to about $600, and from sums added by friends, a $1000 U. S. Bond was purchased for $1196.25. In 1870 this bond was exchanged for thirteen shares of the Ogdensburg and Lake Champlain Rail Road. On July 20, 1871 another hundred dollars was donated to the fund by Mrs. Albert Smith, daughter of Rev. Mr. Chaddock. And on Sept. 4, 1872 another fair was held which realized the sum of $323.36. From a report made by the Treasurer, Dec. 1, 1876 it will be seen that the Alumni Fund at that time amounted to about $2,300, which accrued as follows: Twenty-eight subscriptions, $718. Fairs, 1869 and 1872, $928; R R. Dividends, $468; Savings Bank interest, $217; total $2,331. It was the hope of some of the Committee that the Alumni fund might amount to at least five thousand dollars, and it is further stated by the Treasurer, Wm. C. Bates, that according to his understanding "the wishes of the contributors were that the interest only of the fund should be used for the school, and if at some future time the fund can no longer be used for that purpose, that it shall be given to some educational object of acknowledged merit."

But alas:

> "The best laid schemes of mice and men
> Gang aft a-gley."

Owing to the depression of stocks, the railroad investment proved a sorry one, realizing a loss of $912. The number of scholars naturally lessened by reason of the High Schools being established in all the surrounding and outlying towns, and no adequate support could be furnished to the teachers only as their salaries were eked out by grants from the Alumni fund. Thus there has been paid to the Preceptors of the Academy from 1873 to 1893 inclusive, some $1,800 of the Alumni fund (leaving a balance of between two and three hundred dollars in the Treasurer's hands).* "It is perhaps fair," says our Treasurer, "to claim that our appropriation of $100, or $150, annually for so many years kept the Academy in session many years that otherwise would have been idle."

I think that most of the following new names belong to Miss McRoy's list.

Anna P. Alden, Willie Barton, Anna Baldwin, Mary D. Boylston, Arthur Chamberlain, Alfred H. Downes, Emma Dorr, Hattie L. Eells, Martha P. French, Alice J. Gardner, David P. Hatch, Warren I. Hall, Alice Hunt, Eva Hunt, Alice Harding, Flora J. Magoun, Grace L. Percival, Lillie Paulding, Fred C. Stetson, Henry L. Sweeny, Samuel S. Sylvester, Charles Sturtevant, Eliza S. Sylvester, Hattie Stetson, Flavell

---

*This balance will probably be given to the town for the use of the Public Library.

S. Thomas, Anna Tolman, Emma Thomas, Emily Turner, Isabel E. Witherell.

JAMES WALLACE MCDONALD (1870—71) was born in Bangor, Me., Jan. 26, 1843, and was graduated from Bowdoin College in 1867. After teaching in E. Abington, (now Rockland) he began in the Academy Sept. 5, 1870, with 31 scholars, and left April 24, 1871, before the close of the term to take a High School in So. Abington (now Whitman). The scholars in the Fall term numbered 32 and in Winter 35. It was to his disadvantage, I think, that he followed a popular and greatly admired young lady principal. He was regarded as a good teacher, but his manner or discipline was, as I am told, not entirely pleasing to the school, and perhaps exposed him to small annoyances. Dr. H. L. Sweeny in his above-mentioned historical address spoke of a remarkable belfry episode, and of a fruitless effort with the air-pump to deprive a mouse of the breath of life—which occurrences some of the students may still remember. The same writer also gives a description of a remarkable two-evening exhibition which occurred under this teacher's administration. Mr. McDonald is now and for a long time has been an efficient and popular agent of the Massachusetts Board of Education, and resides in Stoneham.

The following names of new scholars may be regarded in general as belonging to Mr. McDonald.

Thomas J. Brooks, Hattie S. Briggs, Sarah R. Beal, Mary A. Cushman, Charles A. Delano, Percy Douglass, Alice W. Eells, John Flavel, Mary A. Hunt, Mary W. Howes, Lucy A. Howland, George Lawrence, Teresa Locke, Lucy Litchfield, Frank W. Magoun, Edgar W.

Phillips, Edwin P. Phillips, Frank Silver, Arthur Sturtevant, Edward P. Sweeny, Sasie Sylvester, Emma L. Savage, Ellen B. Stetson, Emma A. Stetson, Florence D. Sweeny, Bella Thomas, Walter I. Underwood, Ella J. Vinall, Fred White.

ROLAND HAMMOND (1871), was born in Mattapoisett, Feb. 14, 1842, graduated at Tufts college, July, 1868, obtained the degree of M. D. from Harvard University in 1872, practised medicine in Bellingham until 1882, when he removed to Brockton [Campello] where he now practises his profession. He taught in Gilford Academy during 1868 and '69, and began teaching here May 2, 1871, with 23 scholars, and taught one term. The Fall term was omitted. Mr. Hammond's manner and disposition seem to have been rather the reverse of those of his predecessor, and his scholars, I presume, were pleased with his easier nature and administration. In Bellingham he was chairman of the school committee and superintendent of schools from 1872 to 1882 inclusive, and was also town clerk during 1880, '81 and '82. In Brockton he was also on the school committee in 1886, '87 and '88, and was Justice of the Peace from 1881 to '88 inclusive. In Sept. 25, 1873, he married Mary Lucinda Rockwood, of Bellingham, and, in 1890, had one son, Roland Hammond, Jr., born July 29, 1875. I think he has prepared a genealogical history of the Hammond family.

Perhaps the following new names may be inserted as belonging here.

L. Vernon Briggs, Horace Baker, Nathan Baker, Nellie Barstow, Stella Barstow, Charles Currell, George N. Capell, Fannie M. Cudworth, Hattie Collamore,

Florina M. Collamore, Lydia Collamore, Edwin A.
Damon, Barney E. Dagon, Jennie Ford, Willard Hodge.
Fred Hopkins, John R. Hobill, Victor E. Hobill, Lizzie
Hobill, Nellie Henry, Isadora Hatch, James C. Jones,
Lizzie Magoun, Edward Purcell, Fred Randall, Emma M.
Ramsdell, Annie B. Ramsdell, John H. Stetson, Elliot
Stetson, Arthur T. Simmons, Fred Simmons, George
Stetson, Frank D. Stetson, Nelson M. Stetson, Frank
Sprague, Addie Sprague, Fannie Stetson, Alden D.
Turner, Charles Turner, Albert Torrey, Cleland
Whiting.

REV. TIMOTHY DWIGHT PORTER STONE (1871--74),
son of Rev. Timothy Stone, and named in part from his
uncle, President Ebenezer Porter of Andover Theological Seminary, was born in Cornwall, Ct., July 27, 1811,
fitted for college at Phillips Andover Academy, studied
for two years in Dartmouth, but graduated from Amherst
in 1834, with Henry Ward Beecher. After teaching
in Concord and Plymouth, N. H. he studied at Andover
Theological Seminary and graduated therefrom in
1842. Subsequently he became Principal of Abbott
Female Seminary in Andover, of the Massachusetts
Reform School in Westboro, and of the Connecticut
Normal School, and taught in the Norwich Grammar
school and in several other Schools. In several places
he has been teacher of elocution. He brought recommendations from the Presidents of Dartmouth and
Amherst Colleges and from other high authorities, and
his programme states that "other references could be
furnished in abundance from every section of the
United States." He began teaching here the Winter
term of 1871--2, and taught something over three years

or thirteen terms. The average number of Scholars here is given as thirty-six, the largest fifty, the smallest twenty-five. One Winter he had an evening school of young men which was fairly successful. One who had good means of knowing speaks of him as "an inspiring and successful teacher." He was certainly a teacher of great experience, of large information, and of much capability, but was at times rather eccentric. When teaching here, he at first had the help of some young ladies from abroad, but was afterward assisted by some of his scholars and by his wife who was highly esteemed as a teacher. His wife's maiden name was Susan M. Dickinson, a native of Holliston, and she is still living in Cortland, N. Y., where her son, John Timothy Stone, is settled as a pastor. Her two daughters, as she informs me, still continue the work of teaching. Mr. Stone had been married once previously, but of the first wife and of several grown up and most promising children he had been quite suddenly and most sadly bereaved, and he probably never fully recovered from the shock.

During his stay in Hanover an addition was made to the philosophical apparatus to the amount of over $150, for the payment of which $100 was received from the Alumni fund, and $50 was given by Mrs. Bigelow. From Dr. Sweeny's Historical Address I also learn that a fair was held in 1872 on the Academy grounds which netted about $400, the proceeds being for the benefit of the Alumni fund.

Among the Academy papers we find this resolve:— "That the Directors of the Hanover Academy, in accepting the resignation of Rev. T. D. P. Stone as its Principal, desire to place on record their sense of the industry, fidelity and care for the promotion and improvement of the Academy property, and for the best interests of the institution which characterized the discharge of his duties during the entire period of his labors in this relation."

Mr. Stone was ordained at Holliston, March 1, 1843, and served in the pastorate of several churches, as at Holliston, Amesbury, Marblehead, Stow, and Assabet, and during his stay here he was pastor of the Congregational church in this village. He also found time to write several works for publication. His death occurred in Albany, N. Y., April 11, 1887.

AUGUSTA BRIGGS (CHENEY).

Towards the last of Mr. Stone's teaching here, in 1874, Mrs. Cheney delivered the following spicy poem at the Alumni Reunion. At my urgent request another picture of herself is here presented, taken evidently when she was in one of her merrier moods.

Alumni, 1874.

I've stood before you now so many times,
And offerings gave, of sentimental rhymes,
I thought it well to-night, to change the strain,
And in rude doggerel now "rise to explain;"
For you all know, I have a merry streak
Which prompts me oft in mirthful vein to speak,
Expressing thus the wish, as you may see,
That this our gathering may more jovial be.

And looking 'round, I see on many a face
Glances annihilating time and space,
For aged wrinkles fail to hide the grin,
The youthful impress of the fun within.
There's Tolman, though his hair is growing white,
He's sprightly as a boy, I see to-night,
And I myself, though getting on in years,
Here feel as merry as my young compeers,
And with a smile, my memory recalls
Sad capers cut in Academic halls.
The ancient building, with bell hung in air,
The recitation room, minus a belfry stair,
But trap in ceiling, cunningly displayed,
Tempting young climbers to its secret shade;
Where Nancy and myself, by help of boosting,
Oft ate our dinners, 'neath the rafters roosting;
And talked of beaux, I fear, far more than books,
Of this boy's plainness, or that one's good looks.
Ah! little thought I then, she would forswear her nation,
And French become, by such a close relation.
The bell rope dangled through the ancient Hall,
And many a merry time I now recall,
When from its use most slyly 'twas perverted,
And every bone and sinew we exerted
By nimble use of our extremist pedals,
As champion athletes to obtain a medal:
A swinger stationed was, at either end,
The rope was big, and hard! and Heaven defend
The luckless legs of rythmic time that failed,
Or once in line, before the ordeal quailed.
For let those ponderous strands but hit your heels,
Your laughter changed at once to painful squeals,
And I remember, when my calves showed scars
More numerous, than a veteran's from the wars.

With those old days, most vividly there comes
The stinging satires of Preceptor Holmes,
Who with his tongue, could more effective flay,
Than all the flogging of the present day;
And girls, as well as boys, all got a hit,
And cowed beneath the lash of his sarcastic wit.
Girls when approaching joyous sweet sixteen,
Are just the age to feel such words most keen,

So I recall a day, when negligence confessing,
I stood before him with imperfect lesson.
He glanced at me with a sardonic smile,
The other eye on Henry Hall meanwhile,
And said in voice of thunderous expansion,
"Did you, and Hall, go to the Ball in Hanson?"
And Sarah Collamore, unlucky elf!
Was always bringing down upon herself
His well aimed thrusts against her flippant way,
And nothing was too sharp for him to say.
So one day, in a tone which struck her dumb,
He said, "A great girl with a skull so numb,
Though beaux from all parts of the country come,
She has not wit enough to do that sum."
His arrows flew with never ending aim.
Each culprit pointed out, and called by name,
That one reminded, "that no strange device
Could learn his lessons by Sophia's eyes;"
And Mary, when dismissal was denied,
Was asked, "If Perry waited her outside?"
She, venturing her boldness to display,
Said, "Wish he did, but he don't go our way."
A hundred little incidents I could recall,
Familiar to these present one and all.
But I'll not greedily usurp the time,
Lest I may bore you, with my foolish rhyme.

Not long ago, I saw some witty man,
Had chanced in a directory, the names to scan,
And served them up with such a heap of fun
As scarce seemed possible, he could have done.
So we within these walls, so well defended,
A rather motley crowd have comprehended.
Turners, and Gardners, Dyers, for occupation,
A Carver, and a Cutler, per quotation.
The shipping too has stood financial shocks,
And well built Briggs are still upon the stocks.
And the young Waterman, in spite of all his tacks
May yet be swamped by these same little smacks.

The followers of Walton, have found this location
And angling young men have plied here their vocation
And in our midst have slyly baited hooks

Intent on fishing, far more than their books,
And in spite of laws which their forefathers set,
Both Salmon and Eels have drawn into their nets,
And it would not be strange, if one patiently waits,
If some bigger fish should come after their Bates.

One word ere I close. Though I justly feel pride
In the dear little river, so near my home side,
As it slowly meanders through meadows of green,
The flow of its waters so calm and serene,
Among these old friends no envy I fear,
You can spare us the river long cherished and dear,
And scarce on its banks need seek shady nooks
While the light is reflected, in your beloved Brooks.

Most of the following new names, we think, may be assigned to Rev. Mr. Stone.

Carver Bates, Cora Bourne, Sadie R. Beal, Velma Briggs, Elvena Currell, Lucy Dagon, Emma J. Estes, John Farrar, William H. Farrar, John H. Flavell, E. T. Fogg, Jr., Elmira T. Foster, James Hunt, James Kenedy, Luther Litchfield, Frank W. Magoun, Mary McCurdy, James L. Paul, Charles Rose, Fred Simmons, Ernest T. Sweeny, George Stetson, John Stone, Herbert Stetson, Howard L. Swan, Lizzie G. Stone, Susie D. Stone, Agnes S. Sturtevant, Abbie Stetson, Ella Turner, William H. Webber, Arthur C. Witherell, George C. Whiting.

Mr. JOHN G. KNIGHT (1875-82), the son of Rev. Joel and Jane L. (Gould) Knight, was born in Ipswich, Jan. 20, 1840, educated at the Academy of East Greenwich, R. I., and at Wesleyan University, Middletown, Ct., enlisted for the war in 1863 and was mustered out as Quartermaster-Sergeant at its close. He first taught in Hingham a year and a half, and then, in 1868, became the first teacher of the Hanover High School where he remained nearly seven years. In April, 1875, he commenced teaching in the Academy and resigned in the Summer of 1882, after a service of wenty-nine terms, or a little over seven years,—only two teachers, Messrs. Chaddock and Holmes, having taught here longer than he. For many years he was Secretary and Treasurer of the Plymouth County Teachers' Association, and for ten years he served as member of the School Com-

JOHN G. KNIGHT.

mittee of Hanover. In 1869 he married Harriet J. Gardner of Hingham, and has two sons, Gardner and George W., both born in Hanover. In recent years he has been employed as clerk in the firm of Ezra Phillips and Sons of this town.

During his teaching here, there were held, according to the Treasurer's Records, no less than three "Flower

Shows" (planned originally by Rev. Dr. Brooks), that of 1876 realizing $70.24, while those of the two following years netted $52.22. From the same records I learn that Mr. Knight kept an evening school in 1878 in the Academy, which netted $25, and that $45 was received from the sale of an old piano. During his academic service he had, as he writes me, "two or three very excellent literary entertainments," but as there are no printed programmes of them, no full account of them can now be given. It is a source of regret that this is the case with most of the Celebrations and Exhibitions and Reunions which have almost yearly taken place in the life of the Academy.

Fortunately we can present here a brief poem which Mrs. Cheney gave at the Alumni Reunion of 1880.

Alumni, 1880.

Once more dear Alma Mater for thy sheltering arm,
   Thy weary children turn again to thee,
And come, as in our happy childhood days,
   To crave a blessing at the parent knee.

We lay our joys and sorrows at thy feet,
   Full sure thy heart still beats for us unchilled,
Though sad and disappointed we may come,
   Our youthful aspirations unfulfilled.

And with our best years spent in bootless strife,
   Achieving nothing of our youthful dream,
We find ourselves both old and grey
   Silently drifting down Life's wayward stream.

Who ever does fill out the woof of life,
   Or perfect the original design?
Who looking backward finds naught to regret?
   Or on Time's record finds no faultless line?

Yet not repining, to thy side we come,
   Far more than we deserve, Our Lord has blest.

And though our thankless hearts sometimes rebelled,
His unremitting kindness stands confessed.

And as with joy we gather here to-night,
  And in fond retrospection view the past,
Look in the loving eyes of youthful friends,
  And tenderly join hands in loving clasp,

We feel the lowliest of us has not lived in vain,
  But all some niche have filled, for them the best,
Where each has found for them Life's problem solved,
  And well content, can leave to God the rest.

The following are but a few of the new names* which, as I suppose, should appear in this list, while it doubtless has names which should appear elsewhere, or possibly be wholly omitted.

Addie Alden, Benjamin P. Barstow, Mary E. Baker, Chester Barker, Walter Barnard, Lizzie B. Barker, Annie W. Bates, Everett E. Corthell, Lucy B. Clark, Carrie E. Curtis, Minnie E. Capell, Julia Collamore, L. F. Doane, Mercer Ford, Carrie A. Ford, Josephine Ford, Dennis A. Flavell, Chauncy D. Ford, Angela B.

---

* It will have been observed in the course of this work, that I have generally sought to avoid the frequent repetition of names, and so I have chiefly made mention of *new* names in the different lists. I would again beg those who see many mistakes in these lists to consider the two-fold difficulty I have had, in the almost total absence of catalogues, in making these lists: first, to ascertain the names of scholars, and, secondly, to give these names their right place. The doing of this latter, especially, has been largely a matter of conjecture, and I have no doubt that many will wonder, smile, or frown, to see their names, if perchance I have these right, so far removed from their proper location. My only hope is that these lists, imperfect as they are, will serve to indicate in a general way something of the numbers and character of those who were accustomed to attend the Academy in its later years. I am certain of one thing, that these lists will be more satisfactory to others, however much dissatisfied they may be, than they are to myself.

Ford, Edith G. Ford, Frank E. Hunt, Ella Josselyn, Charles H. Knapp, Ella B. Keene, Walter Keene, Clara Lindsay, Nellie Loving, Louise Loving, Jason A. Magoun, Joseph C. Otis, Daniel Phillips, Edmund Packard, Solomon P. Russell, Lucy Russell, Grace L. Russell, Ruthetta M. Sylvester, Emily E. Sylvester, Martha W. Sylvester, Agnes Sherman, Grace Stetson, Etta M. Stetson, Martin Simmons, Lydia D. Stetson, Susie Simmons, A. V. Tillson, Susan O. Turner, Walter R. Torrey, Howard Torrey, George Torrey, Lillie Totman, Harriet Tolman, Alfred Tolman, Ruth Turner, Samuel A. Walker, George H. Whitman, Charlotte E. Winslow, Lina White, Harry Winslow.

FRANK WALLACE BRETT

FRANK WALLACE BRETT (1882—88), born in Hingham, May 14, 1861, was graduated from the Hingham

High School, and, in 1880, from the Bridgewater Normal School. After teaching in Norwell Centre about a year and a half, he became preceptor of Hanover Academy September, 1882, and resigned in June, 1888, his term of Academic teaching amounting to six years, being in comparison with that of others the fourth in duration. The school increased in numbers until the average attendance exceeded 40, and the membership exceeded 50 per year, while his income as teacher, (with help from the Alumni fund, presumably) averaged $750 a year, and in the last year amounted to $925. During his administration, (in 1886) a great work was done in repairing and fitting up the Academy at an expense of over $500, for the payment of which $150 was received from Mrs. Bigelow, $100 from Mrs. Salmond, and $271 from the Barstow Fund. The Hanover Brass Band, by its rent of the hall, lent a helping hand to the furtherance of the interests of the Academy.

While teaching in Hanover Mr. Brett took to himself a wife. In August 2, 1885, he married Annie Josephine Cuming, and has had two sons, Afley Leonel, born August 9, 1887, and Roy Cuming, born August 22, 1891, both of whom are living.

Mr. Brett, more than other teachers, seems to have patterned somewhat after college examples. I refer to his occasional issuance of catalogues or leaflets, containing the scholars' names. So far as I have seen, Mr. George Conant is the only other teacher who has done so. Then he advertises a fixed course of study, at the end of which is a graduation with its salutatory, valedictory, etc. Four such graduation programmes I have seen each ending off with a Latin motto, perhaps not always patterned after the highest style of Ciceronian

Latinity), and two of these, referring to the years 1886 and 1887, required each an all-day performance. In the former case there were two graduates, Georgie Ellen Barstow, and Hattie Mabel Chandler, and an Alumni oration pronounced by William Paley Duncan, Esq., in which he gave a very full account of the school for the past thirty years, and many reminiscences of his school days*. We herewith give the opening and the close of his address as printed in a local sheet.

"Mr. President, fellow Alumni, and former classmates:

Although I wish this honor had fallen to another, I yet most gratefully participate in the anniversary exercises and reunion of the Alumni of our ancient Academy. I welcome you back to the classic shades of our Alma Mater on this bright day of leafy June. I welcome you Elders freighted with life's successes, with honor and position; I welcome you whose life has not so smoothly onward run, who have encountered the rough edges of disappointment, whose bright hopes have not been fully realized. And you I welcome who to-day, just now, have entered our ranks, you newly fledged Alumni, full of fond expectations, ambitious thought

---

*In a recent letter he mentions this reminiscence: "We had a Debating Club composed largely of students of the Academy. The question for debate one evening was on this wise: 'Which is the greater sinner, the drunkard or the moderate drinker?' After listening to a labored argument on one side that the moderate drinker was by far the greater offender, a well known disputant on the opposite side. [Mr. James Turner, I should think] arose and said: 'Mr. President, if the argument of the gentleman is true that the moderate drinker is the greater sinner, I should advise that all of us moderate drinkers become drunkards in order to improve our morals.' Suffice it to say that the debate was decided in his favor."

and purpose. Brothers, sisters, teachers, friends, robust, victorious, weary or disheartened, beginners, or just ending life's drama, one and all, I bid you welcome, yea, thrice welcome, on this festal day."

The closing part was as follows:

"But, fellow Alumni, I forbear. In theory we are all young, but as we gaze the truth begins to dawn upon many of us that the boon of youth is ours no longer. Yet, as we strike hands to-day in love and friendship, we forget

> The strife of manhood with its hopes and fears,
> The griefs and trials of our riper years.
> The sad experience and the sore defeat,
> The prayer unanswered, the triumph incomplete.
>
> Our minds revert to golden days of yore,
> In sweetest retrospect we count them o'er.
> And deem each gentle face, each manly form
> As fair, as brave as though unswept by storm;
> As bright and beautiful as erst in youth,
> By sin unsullied, radiant with truth.
>
> So let us part with many a fond regret,
> Hoping to meet again as we have met,
> In heaven or earth--what matter if we love,
> In spirit one--on earth or realms above."

In the evening there was a Social Reunion which was enlivened by the Hanover Brass Band and made edifying and interesting by divers addresses of distinguished Alumni.

In 1887 there were four graduates with another Alumni Oration. As it may interest some to see a specimen programme I will venture to print the following:

GRADUATING EXERCISES, JUNE 17, 1887, AT 10 A.M.

SALUTATORY—"Aims,"   Ernest Alonzo Thomas
READING—"Piece of Calico,"   Viola May Bryant

DUET —   Misses M. A. Farrar and A. N. Little
READING—"The Engineer's Murder,"   L. P. Rose
CLASS HISTORY—"For, Four, Forth,"   Annie Niles Little
LATIN ESSAY—"Lingua et Scientia,"   Mabel Allen Farrar
READING—"The Old Surgeon's Story,"   I. M. Fernald
VALEDICTORY—"Education and Learning."   .   Mary Ellen Curtis
            PRESENTATION OF DIPLOMAS.

            DINNER—BASKET COLLATION.

        ALUMNI ORATION AND ADDRESSES, AT 2 P.M.
                "Education of To-Day."
                FLAVEL S. THOMAS, M.S.
                    OF HANSON, MASS.
                SOCIAL REUNION AT 8 P.M
                Reading and Vocal Music.

The next year the graduating exercises were held in the evening. There were three graduates, Viola May Bryant, Mary Ellen McCarthy, Nettie May Chandler, but no Alumni Oration. I know of no other printed graduation programme (though there may have been others) save that of 1891, the last year but one of the Academy's existence.

After leaving Hanover, Mr. Brett taught as Principal in the Avery Grammar School at Highlandville, in Needham, for three and a half years, and then took charge of a new large Grammar School in Braintree for some four years, when he resigned to enter upon the practice of medicine in South Braintree, having obtained in 1894 the degree of M. D. from the college of Physicians and Surgeons in Boston. While teaching in Braintree he was for several Winters a sub-master of the Brockton Evening High School. He has also since served on the School Committee of Braintree.

At his graduation from the Medical School, the Trustees appointed him lecturer on the faculty, and he has since held continuously the chair of Bacteriology in that Institution. Much of his success in life he "attributes to the healthy stimulus of the vigorous young minds with whom he was so pleasantly brought in contact during the six long-to-be-remembered years in Hanover Academy."

The following is mainly a memory list of new names, as given principally by Mr. Brett.

Lena B. Allen, Lottie W. Brownville, Viola M. Bryant, Edward C. Bowers, Florence M. Barnard, Bertha L. Buttrick, Edward K. Bacon, Charles D. Bonney, Clarence E. Barnard, William Curtis, Edgar Chandler, Ellen F. Cox, Hattie M. Chandler, Henrietta Collamore, Nellie D. Collamore, Mary E. Curtis, Nettie N. Chandler, Joseph M. Christy, Ellen B. Curtis, Percy Damon, Harry Damon, Jennie Drew, Edwin Damon, Elwin Damon, Alice Dow, Emma Dame, Edward R. Flavell, Mabel A. Farrar, Ida M. Fernald, Ella R. Flavell, Lillian C. Flavell, Edgar C. Gardner, Henry Gardner, Nellie N. Howland, Samuel W. Hollis, Grace F. Hatch, Marcellus Hatch, Walter R. Hatch, Annie A. Howland, Oliver Hatch, Hiram H. Howland, Albert C. Joyce,, John F. Kirby, John Kalua, Annie N. Little, Everett S. Lawrence, Lacie B. Magoun, William Merritt, Lucy J. McFarlen, Mary E. McCarthy, Arthur Magoun, Sadie F. Merritt, Annie Mann, William Pratt, George T. Reeves, Elizabeth P. Rose, Frederic S. Smith, Sarah E. Snell, Delia A. Studley, Nellie Simmons, Fannie W. Stetson, Flora E. Smith, S. Eliza Snell, Fred S. Smith, Mertie C. Simmons, William W. Sylvester, William Turner, Nellie Tower, Jennie Tower, Henry Tolman, Sadie E. Tolman, Ernest A. Thomas, Herbert C. Tolman, Burton L. Thomas, Emma S.

Thayer, Maria W. Tolman, Joseph Tolman, Thomas E. Waterman, Harry T. Watkins, Thomas S. Walker, George E. Waterman, Alberta White, Osmund F. White.

ANDREW PRESTON AVERILL (1888—'89), was born in Middleton, Essex County, July 18, 1856, graduated at Harvard, 1882, taught as principal in the High School, in Bolton, in Townsend, and in the Sawin Academy and Dowse High School at Sherborn, which is his last known address. He was preceptor of Hanover Academy the Fall and Winter terms of 1888—'89*. His brief term of service here does not seem to have been eminently successful. The school, for some cause, lacked interest in their studies.

In 1890 he writes to his class Secretary, Henry W. Cunningham of Boston, that his "life has been uneventful as a teacher in the public schools of Eastern Massachusetts." In some respects his life has not been without events. Soon after graduation he married Miss Clara Ada McKay, in New York city, and up to 1895 has had five children, the first of whom was "class baby," that is, the first child of a member of the class born after graduation, and, as such, little "Charlie Peabody" received a cradle from the class.

MRS. ELLEN JOSEPHINE (TOWLE) SWEENY (1889—90), belonging to a family of Scotch descent, was the daughter of Darius and Hannah (Dimond) Towle, and was born in N. Danville, N. H., June 20, 1850. When four-

---

*Under Mr. Averill's administration and thereafter, there were but three school terms per year, while hitherto there had been four. Mr. Brett, the preceding teacher inaugurated a partial change by shortening the summer term to seven weeks.

teen years of age, as she writes me, a copy of "The Good Girl and True Woman" fell into her hands, and from that time her heart was set upon taking a course of study at Mary Lyon's school. As a result of that purpose she in 1876 graduated from Mt. Holyoke Seminary.

Immediately upon graduating she became Preceptress of the Seminary in Doylestown, Pa. Subsequent-

MRS. SWEENY.

ly she taught in the West School of Malden two years, and then became principal of the Medfield high school, which position she resigned in 1884 to become the wife of Dr. Henry L. Sweeny, of Hanover. A few years after she opened a private school in her house for the younger children of the village, teaching them largely after the kindergarten method. After a year and a half of this service, she was induced to take the principalship of the Academy, and held this office from April, 1889, to November, 1890. Miss Mary Ellen Curtis was happily chosen by her as assistant, while her own husband lectured to the school two days each week upon Chemistry, Geology and Philosophy. Mrs. Sweeny was an enthusiastic teacher, and had the happy faculty of interesting her students and enlisting their sympathies in the work. Since making her home in Kingston, N. H., she has been largely engaged in church, missionary, and literary work. For several years she has been a correspondent of the *Exeter News Letter*. With restored health and pleasant surroundings, she has every reason to hope for many years of usefulness and rational enjoyment. During her academic service in Hanover, a commemorative exercise was held, July 10, 1889, consisting of a Word of Greeting by the assistant teacher, Mary E. Curtis, the reading of Rev. Mr. Dyer's Dedicatory Address by Mr. J. G. Knight, singing of the original dedicatory hymns, and a carefully prepared History of the Academy by Dr. Henry L. Sweeny. I recollect also a Bryant Day celebration as a most inspiring occasion, when the students in their performances showed a fine appreciation of Nature's great poet.

Miss EVANGELINE HATHAWAY (1890—92), daughter of Rev. James Hathaway, was born in Jackson, Me., Jan. 21, 1869, but spent her earliest years in Bangor. She was fitted for college in a private school at Portland, was graduated from Wellesley in 1890, began teaching at the Academy the winter term of 1890, and ended June 24, 1892. In a letter received from her she says: "The Academy always will be dear to me because it was my first school, and because I feel that I came into closer sympathy with my students than I have ever done since." After leaving Hanover she became for two years principal of the Somerset High School, and then went abroad for a year and studied at Oxford, England. After her return she taught for a time in New Bedford, and subsequently in Boston in Volkemann Preparatory School for Boys. Her present address is Woodfords, Me. I think Miss H. gave several public

MISS EVANGELINE HATHAWAY.

entertainments in the Academy, but the one I most distinctly recollect was given in the Odd Fellows Hall the evening of June 20, 1892, and consisted in the performance of a Farce, "Wanted — A Male Cook," and a Play called a "Rainy Evening," written by Mrs. Dr. French of Hanover; the proceeds of which entertainment were to be devoted to repairs for the Academy.

The following named misses took part in the play: Ella Groce, Lottie and Annie Whiting, Florence Barker, Annie Bryant, Bertha Hatch, Lottie Turner, Lucy Litchfield, Edith Waterman. The performers of the Farce were Chester Turner, Byron Merrill, Ernest Howard, and Newton Litchfield.

The last graduating exercises of Hanover Academy took place on the evening of June 26, 1891, in Odd Fellows Hall. The two graduates, Mary Ellen Clapp and Bertha Louise Buttrick, both of Norwell, had for their class motto: "Onward and Upward." The principal exercises of the occasion consisted in Singing, by Miss Bertha Barker, an invited guest from Wellesley, and by Mr. John E. Burgess; Reading by Miss Florence Barker; Recitation by Rudolph W. Sweeny and James C. Waterman; and Essays by Misses Clapp and Buttrick, the respective subjects of which were: "Life, its Successes and Failures," and, "Moral and Intellectual Development." Diplomas were presented by Rev. D. B. Ford, and prayer was offered and benediction pronounced by Rev. F. S. Harraden, Rector of St. Andrew's Church.

We here subjoin a list of names (not hitherto mentioned) of those who attended school during the last years of the Academy's life, and more especially during the administration of the two last-named teachers.

Florence S. Barker, Lucy Barricau, Annie Bryant, Mary E. Clapp, Catherine Christy, Fred Capel, Anna M. Davenport, Nettie Damon, Charles Gassett, Fred Gillett, Edward Goodrich, Ella B. Groce, Parker Hill, Oliver Hatch, Charles Howland, Ernest Howard, Joseph R. Hatch, Hester Howland, Bertha J. Hatch, Mabel M. Howland, Hattie Johnson, Teresa Kent,

Newton Litchfield, Harvey LeFurgy, Lucy E. Litchfield, Ida Lord, Louis McMillan, Byron H. Merrill, Essie Magoun, Rudolph W. Sweeny, Francis B. Sylvester, Lottie F. Turner, Lucy Turner, Elliot Turner, Charles Torrance, Chester W. Turner, James C. Waterman, Bessie Wild, Ellen Wild, Edith Waterman, Mildred Waterman, Lottie Whiting, Annie Whiting, Maud Whiting, John Whyman, William Whyman.

PART IV.

MISCELLANEA.

For the sake of convenient reference we give here a list of the Academy Teachers with approximate dates of their teaching.

REV. CALVIN CHADDOCK   1808-18.

ZEPHANIAH A. BATES	1828	CHARLES A. REED	1856-60
HORACE H. ROLFE	1829	SAMUEL G. STONE	1860-1
REV. CYRUS HOLMES	1830	PELEG T. KEENE	1861-4
ETHAN ALLEN	1830	ARTHUR S. LAKE	1864-5
REV. CALVIN WOLCOTT	1831	ISAIAH DOLE	1865
JOHN P. WASHBURN	1832	JOHN P. APTHORP	1865-6
DR. IRA WARREN	1833	PETER L. WOODBURY	1866-7
THOMAS F. WHITE	1834-7	EBENEZER B. GAY	1867
HERMAN BOURN	1837-8	JOHN P. THORNDYKE	1867-8
HANNAH W. JOHNSON	1837	JOSEPHINE MCROY	1869-70
JOSIAH FULLER AND SISTER	1838-9	JAMES W. MCDONALD	1870-1
REV. CYRUS HOLMES	1840-8	ROLAND HAMMOND	1871
MARY F. TAGGARD	1847-51	REV. T. D. P. STONE	1871-5
CHARLES HITCHCOCK	1848-9	JOHN G. KNIGHT	1875-82
GEORGE T. WOLCOTT	1849	FRANK W. BRETT	1882-8
MARTIN P. MCLAUTHLIN	1850-4	ANDREW P. AVERILL	1888-9
GEORGE CONANT AND WIFE,	1854-5	ELLEN J. SWEENY	1889-90
FREDERIC O. BARSTOW	1855-6	EVANGELINE HATHAWAY	1890-2

Of the above teachers the following were College or Seminary graduates:

From Dartmouth: Calvin Chaddock, H. H. Rolfe, Peter L. Woodbury, A. S. Lake, Charles Hitchcock.*

*Mr. Holmes, though not a graduate, was a student for some time at Dartmouth, and his daughter has in her possession letters written to him by his distinguished classmate, Hon. Salmon P. Chase, who graduated in 1826.

HISTORY OF HANOVER ACADEMY.   149

From Brown University: Ethan Allen, Herman Bourn, George T. Wolcott, Frederic O. Barstow.
From Amherst: T. D. P. Stone, J. P. Apthorp, Chas. A. Reed, S. G. Stone.
From Harvard: Zephaniah A. Bates, A. P. Averill.
From Bowdoin: Isaiah Dole, J. W. McDonald.
From Tufts: Roland Hammond.
From Phillips Andover Academy: Calvin Wolcott, M. P. McLauthlin.
From Wesleyan University: J. G. Knight.
From Mt. Holyoke: Ellen J. Sweeny.
From Wellesley: Evangeline Hathaway.
From Framingham Normal School: Josephine McRoy.
From Bridgewater Normal School: F. W. Brett.

ACADEMY TRUSTEES, 1828.

Alexander Wood, Horatio Cushing, John B. Barstow, Col. Samuel Tolman, Jr., and Horace Collamore.

ACADEMY TRUSTEES, 1852—61.

Samuel Salmond, Rev. Samuel Cutler, Rev. Abel G. Duncan, Dr. Alfred C. Garratt, Seth Barker, Capt. Elijah Barstow, Robert Sylvester, Melzar Hatch, Isaac H. Haskins, Rev. Joel Mann, Stephen Josselyn, Rev. Joseph Freeman, Rev. James Aiken, Thomas H. C. Barstow.

ACADEMY DIRECTORS (subsequent to incorporation).

Rev. Samuel Cutler, Rev. Joseph Freeman, Elijah Barstow, Isaac H. Haskins, Lemuel C. Waterman, T. H. C. Barstow, Nathaniel Barstow, Edward F. Wood, Dr. Woodbridge R. Howes, Benjamin B. Torrey, Isaac M. Wilder, Edmund Q. Sylvester, Warren Wright, Rev.

Dr. William H. Brooks, Rudolphus C. Waterman, D. B. Ford, Rev. Frank S. Harraden, J. Williams Beal, Joseph S. Sylvester. (Several of these have also served as clerks and as treasurers).

Three of the above enumerated Directors, Messrs. Cutler, Brooks and Ford have served as Presidents of the Board, said Board ever consisting of six members elected by the Proprietors.

REV. SAMUEL CUTLER

No history of Hanover Academy can pass over in silence the name of REV. SAMUEL CUTLER, who for a score of years served as President of the Board. He was the son of Samuel and Lydia (Prout) Cutler, and was born in Newburyport, May 12, 1805, and in early life was engaged in business in Portland, Me., and in Boston. In 1836, at the age of 29, he began to prepare for the ministry, and was settled over St. Andrew's

Church at Hanover Corners for some thirty years, from Nov., 1841, to March, 1872. He then removed to Boston where he died July 17, 1880. His remains now rest in our Hanover Cemetery.

During his stay in Hanover occurred the great trouble and sorrow of the nation's life in its civil war, and also the very serious trouble in the life of the Academy, whose interests ever lay closely on his mind and heart, and to whose welfare he gave in unstinted measure his time and thought and care. Mr. Cutler was a man in whose character and conduct there was nothing light or frivolous. Life, right, and duty were with him very serious matters. While always polite and affable, he, I think, never could have been jovial in society or as a companion. His regard for real attainments and solid worth made him averse to all pretence and show and insincerity. From a course which seemed right to his conscientious convictions nothing could deter him or turn him aside. Evidence of this may be seen in the partial change of his ecclesiastical relations which in his later years he felt it his duty to make, yet at a cost whose greatness cannot easily be imagined.

Amid his multifarious labors he found time to write a number of small volumes, several of which were published by the American Tract Society. Perhaps the most noted of these is the one entitled "The Name above Every Name."

The above portrait of Rev. Mr. Cutler was paid for by the Dorcas Society of St. Andrew's Church.

Another revered and greatly beloved name, which Hanover and its Academy will ever delight to honor, is that of REV. WILLIAM HENRY BROOKS, S. T. D. He was born in Baltimore, Jan. 11, 1831. After graduating from the Episcopal Theological Seminary in Va. he was ordained in the historic Christ Church in Alexandria of which Washington had been Vestryman. He served in the pastorates of Newark, Del., Lenox, Mass., Brockport, N. Y., Plymouth and Webster, and then came to Hanover as Rev. Mr. Cutler's successor in the Spring of 1872. Here he remained until the Autumn

REV WILLIAM HENRY BROOKS.

of 1888 when he removed to Boston. He is now and has been for some 34 years the honored Secretary of the Mass. Diocesan Convention. For some 16 years he served as President of the Academy Board of Directors and to this service gave much of time and thought. Dr. Brooks was deservedly popular with his fellow citizens, being highly esteemed both for his solid attainments and his social qualities. More than once he was chosen representative to our State Legislature. Though he may be called a Southerner by birth and ties of kindred, he was always a Union man, and he took especial interest in the raising of the soldiers' monument; and perhaps the proudest day of his life was when he served as President of the Day at its dedication. The pamphlet which he subsequently prepared, giving a full account of the interesting exercises of that occasion, is itself a worthy monument of his devotion to the highest interests of his town and country.

ALUMNI WHO HAVE STUDIED MEDICINE.

Joseph E. Corlew, Daniel C. Otis, Francis Collamore, George A. Collamore, Joshua James Ellis, Frederic O. Barstow, Flavel S. Thomas, Marcus Ames, Charles P. French, Clarence L. Howes, Henry L. Sweeny, Benjamin P. Barstow, L. Vernon Briggs.*

JOSEPH E. CORLEW, while attending the Academy, lived with his parents in the "Wild Cat" district of So. Scituate, near Studley Hill, in a house which is now torn down. He obtained the degree of M. D. from Harvard University in 1842 and practised first in Wiscasset, Me. then in Millbury, Mass., and finally in So. Weymouth, where he died in 1864. Some of his Academy schoolmates who were most intimately acquainted with him, deemed him a man of ready, popular, and almost brilliant talents. His son, Joseph T. Corlew, is also one of our Academy Alumni and has taught in our public schools.

---

*This and other lists which follow have reference mainly to the later history of the Academy.

DANIEL C. OTIS, was born in So. Scituate in 1826, studied in Hanover Academy under Mr. Holmes, and subsequently at the Tremont Medical School, Boston. After obtaining his diploma he settled in Providence and died there at the age of 32. He was never married.

FRANCIS COLLAMORE.

FRANCIS COLLAMORE, son of Horace and Laura (Briggs) Collamore, and a descendant of the distinguished Dr. Jeremiah Hall, was born in N. Pembroke, Dec. 7, 1825. After leaving the Academy and teaching for a time, he began the study of medicine with his uncle, Dr. Anthony Collamore, and in 1847 graduated from the medical department of Dartmouth College. His subsequent life has been spent in his native town where he has practised his profession and also has filled many important town offices, having been town-clerk for twelve years, a member of the School Committee for over thirty years, also Town Treasurer, and Treasurer of the Marshfield Agricultural Society. He has also had much to do in the settling of estates. In 1881 he was a member of the State Legislature. Probably no one in Pembroke is better versed in its history than he, and his historical writings should erelong be made to see the light of day. It is an interesting circumstance that his father before him was also an Academy student, a pupil of "Parson Chaddock."

We may add that a daughter of his, Florina M. Collamore, one of our Academy girls, has likewise served several years as a member of the School Committee in Pembroke.

In this connection I may speak of LEANDER COLLAMORE, a brother of Dr. Francis Collamore, who studied at the Academy under Mr. Holmes, and at Phillips Exeter Academy, and was graduated at Dartmouth College in 1856. It is my impression that he had the law in view, but in the exciting times of the Kansas crusade and "border ruffianism" he went to Lawrence, and after residing there some eighteen months, died on Sept. 9, 1859, aged 26 years.

It is an interesting circumstance that a cousin of his, George W. Collamore, for a time Mayor of Lawrence, was smothered to death in his own well wherein his wife concealed him during the raid led on by Quantrell, who searched the premises for him in vain, but set his house on fire.

GEORGE A. COLLAMORE, son of Dr. Anthony and Caroline (Hatch) Collamore, was born in Pembroke, November 9, 1833, graduated from Dartmouth in 1854, taught in Virginia, studied medicine at Dartmouth College and Harvard University Medical School, graduating from this last mentioned school in 1859. He served as surgeon in our Civil War, and is now a practising physician in Toledo, Ohio. I may state that several sisters of his have attended the Academy, the names of whom are given under the head of school teachers. The Academy has always been remarkably well patronized by the Collamore families of North Pembroke.

JOSHUA JAMES ELLIS was born in Boston, September 13, 1826, but while an Academy student he made his home in North Marshfield at the house of a relative, Daniel Phillips, Esq. He was a bright and good-looking boy, and must in very early life have often been placed upon a table or other platform to speak his little pieces —so self-possessed and so pleasing was he as a speaker in our Academy days and in after years. He was graduated at Brown University in 1847, and at Harvard Medical school in 1852. In 1847—8, he taught a private school in Newport, R. I., where he married, in 1852, a daughter of Rev. Dr. John O. Choules. After practising as a physician in Bristol, R. I., 1854—62, he became assistant surgeon in Mass. Volunteers, 1862—63. He died at Newport, March 17, 1863.

FLAVELL SHURTLEFF THOMAS.

FLAVEL SHURTLEFF THOMAS was born in Hanson, September 7, 1852, and on leaving its town schools studied at Hanover Academy, Phillips Andover Academy, Harvard University, and about a dozen other of the higher institutions of our land. He obtained his M. D. from Harvard in 1874, and after practising a few months in Ithaca, N. Y., he returned to Hanson, where he has resided ever since. In 1879 he married Caroline M. Smith, and has two children, Perry Shurtleff and Saba Drew. In 1892 he received the degree of LL. D. from Shurtleff College. To enumerate all the works he has written and all the honorary titles he has received would, I think, even in diamond type, more than fill up one of these pages, and hence, for a full account of these things and of the offices he has filled, we must refer our readers to his biography, which is found in the "History of Plymouth County," and in the Plymouth County "Biographical Review." Of our Academic students we may say that many have done nobly, but thou, at least in certain lines, hast excelled them all.

CHARLES P. FRENCH, son of Dr. John O. French, formerly a practising physician in this village, studied at the Dartmouth Medical school, and was settled in Duxbury, Truro and Pembroke, but is now retired from practice.

CLARENCE L. HOWES, son of Dr. Woodbridge R. Howes, who was for many years a popular and successful physician in this place, was born at Mattapoisett, March 24, 1848, fitted for college in our Academy under Mr. Lake, and graduated from Amherst in 1869. After teaching in Pembroke, in Spencertown Academy, Austerlitz, N. Y., and in the High School of Rockland, he entered the Institute of Technology in Boston, and graduated therefrom in 1873 with the degree of B. S. He then engaged in civil engineering and surveying till 1876, when he began the study of medicine and at the same time taught for one year in the Eliot Grammar and Boston Latin schools. Afterward he attended medical lectures at Dartmouth college and at the Long Island College Hospital, where, in 1878, he received the degree of M. D. In the same year, October 3, he was married to Mary O. Hapgood of Worcester, and since then has resided in Hanover. He has had two children, a son and a daughter—the latter alone surviving. For nearly a score of years he has served as Chairman of the School Committee.

HENRY L. SWEENY.

HENRY L. SWEENY, the eldest son of Edward M. and Lucy (Thaxter) Sweeny, was born in Bridgewater, Apr. 3, 1858. At an early age his parents moved to Hanson near the tack manufactory of Ezra Phillips and Sons, in whose employ his father has been connected from that time to the present. In 1870 they again moved to the George Curtis place in Hanover where they still reside. On the opening of the railroad to Hanover Corners in 1868 he began to attend the Academy and continued there under the tuition of Miss McRoy, Mr. McDonald and Rev. Mr. Stone. In the last year of his attendance he served as Mr. Stone's assistant. In January, 1875, he entered Adams Academy at Quincy and graduated there in 1878. Soon after entering Harvard College he was obliged to leave on account of poor health. In 1879 he entered the Harvard Medical School from which he graduated in 1882. He first began to practise in Kingston N. H. for a short time, then for about a year in the city of Boston, after which, in 1883, he came to Hanover, taking for the first winter the practice of the late Dr. John O. French while the latter was in Florida. He remained in Hanover until 1890 when he returned to Kingston, N. H., where he still resides. Dr. Sweeny has served as member of the School Board and as Town Clerk, for three years each, is now a Justice of the Peace, a member of the local Board of Health, and County physician for Rockingham County. He is also a member of the New Hampshire Medical Society, the New Hampshire Associated Boards of Health, and of the American Medical Association.

In 1884 Dr. Sweeny, as we have already stated, married Ellen Josephine Towle, who afterwards became Principal of Hanover Academy, and during her term of service he was assistant in the school. Thus at two different periods he has served as assistant teacher in the Academy "in which he has passed many pleasant and happy days, and none could regret the passing away of the old institution more than he."

BENJAMIN PARKER BARSTOW.

BENJAMIN PARKER BARSTOW, was born in Duxbury, Aug. 31, 1860, entered Hanover Academy in 1876 and graduated from Boston University School of Medicine June, 1882. He was first settled in Exeter, N. H., and in 1884 came to Kingston where he has lived and practised ever since. His practice, I believe, is after the Homœopathic method. In June, 1885, he married Helen B. Steele of Epsom, N. H., and has two children.

L. VERNON BRIGGS.

We may state that Mr. L. VERNON BRIGGS, who amid multifarious cares and duties has for some years past paid considerable attention to the healing art, is now taking at Dartmouth College a thorough course of medical instruction. In Academy matters and in Town matters he has ever manifested a deep interest, and his printed volumes of Ship-building Records, of Church Records, of Cemetery Records, and of Town Records, are a monument to his indefatigable industry and public spirit. For many years he was President of our Alumni Association. For the many other offices he has held or still holds, the reader is referred to his "Church and Cemetery Records," pp. 54, 55.

Our readers must be given to understand that in some of the above biographical notices we have not told and could not bear to tell the whole truth. From more than one instance of a seriously marred life comes especially the solemn warning not to touch, nor taste, nor handle.

ALUMNI WHO HAVE BECOME LAWYERS.

George M. Reed, Franklin E. Felton, Charles Hitchcock, Edward G. Stetson, Charles F. Phillips, John S. Crosby, William P. Duncan, Walter R. Torrey.

GEO. MILTON REED, brother of the teacher, Charles A. Reed, was born in Weymouth, Jan. 8, 1840, fitted for college in Weymouth and Hanover, graduated from Amherst in 1862, taught school in 1862—3, and then studied in the Harvard Law School. He resides in Boston, and since 1871 has been Law reporter of decisions of the Courts for the Boston Daily Advertiser.

FRANKLIN ELIOT FELTON, half brother of President Felton of Harvard College, was graduated from Harvard in 1851, was subsequently made A. M. without further study, and in 1853 received the degree of LL. B. His last known address was Baltimore, Maryland.

EDWARD GRAY STETSON, son of Rev. Caleb Stetson of So. Scituate, formerly of Medford, graduated from Cambridge College in 1853, and subsequently from Harvard Law School. After graduation he received from his college the degree of A. M. without further study, and in 1868 the degree of LL. B. For nearly 30 years past he has been practising law in San Francisco, Cal.

CHARLES FOLLEN PHILLIPS, son of Ezra Phillips, was born in Hanson, April 21, 1846, and died Jan. 30, 1885. After graduating from the Boston University Law School, June, 1873, he acted for a short time as Assistant Register of Probate for Middlesex County till his health failed him. Besides going to the South in the Winter of 1874, he twice made a visit to Europe.

WILLIAM PALEY DUNCAN, son of Rev. Abel G. Duncan*, was born April 1, 1831, studied at Williston Seminary and at Amherst College, spent the early part of his life in teaching in Maine, Michigan, and Massachusetts, and after admission to the bar opened an office in Boston. He married Abbie F. Crane, of Freetown, and has had three children, two of whom, John F. and Payson Williston, are living. Mr. Duncan, like his honored father, has the poetic genius, but ill health does not now allow him to take any lofty or long flights with his Pegasus. We have already given a specimen of his verse in a previous page, and he has kindly consented to furnish for our work a few closing lines. Our readers will find in the Pamphlet of the Soldiers' Monument, page 82, a touching tribute by him to the "Unknown" ones of our buried soldiers in the sunny South.

WILLIAM P DUNCAN

*Rev. Mr. Duncan, a man of distinguished ability and genius, and helper of all educational work, was for many years an honored Director of Hanover Academy. He came to Hanover Aug., 1833, as pastor of the Centre Church, resigned his pastorate April, 1854, and died in Hanover April 23, 1874. For some six years he represented the Town in our State Legislature. His two daughters, Laura J. King, of North Adams, and Lucia A. Dean, of Taunton, have both deceased. These are the "tall daughters" whom Miss Taggard mentions as among her pupils.

WALTER R. TORREY was born in So. Scituate, April 1, 1864, studied at the Academy under Mr. Knight, and subsequently attended the Bryant and Stratton school, and Boston University.

WALTER R. TORREY

He studied law with Judge Hosea Kingman and at Boston University Law School, was admitted to the Bar June, 1896, and is now associated with Judge Kingman in practice. In his vocation he has been very successful, and has recently won the most important cases ever tried in Plymouth County, known as the "Hull Official Bribery Cases." His principal business is in this County, and in the cities of Boston and New York. At present he is counsel for the towns of Scituate and Hull, and is interested in the management of several large trust estates and corporations. He has also been largely engaged in real estate and mercantile transactions in this State and in New Jersey. While his home is in Norwell, he has a summer residence at North Scituate Beach, a beautiful place near the "Glades," which he has done very much to develop, having built there himself more than twenty houses. In 1895 his town gave him a majority vote for Representative. He confesses to have amassed already quite a fortune, and, if he keeps on financially as he has begun, he bids fair to become our Alumni Rockefeller.

He married Helen H., only daughter of Hon. Ebenezer T. Fogg, late deceased, and has one son, Wendell.

I may state that several of the Torrey name and kindred who were once members of our Academy have likewise been remarkably successful in business.

Mr. Barry, on page 98 of his History of Hanover, makes mention of Isaiah Wing, a native of Hanover, who, according to report, was one of Mr. Chaddock's pupils after he was a married man. Subsequently he studied law, and after practising here for a time moved to Cincinnati, O., where he died.

Alumni Who Have Entered the Ministry.

Marcus Ames, William Henry Stetson, D. B. Ford, Frederic O. Barstow, George A. Litchfield, David P. Hatch, William C. Litchfield, James C. Church, Ernest A. Thomas.

REV MARCUS AMES

MARCUS AMES, son of Azel and Mercy (Hatch) Ames, was born in Marshfield, Feb. 26, 1828, studied at Phillips Andover Academy, being the valedictorian of his class, also at Williams College, in Harvard Medical School, and in New York College of Physicians and Surgeons, graduating in 1853.

After studying Theology with Rev. Erastus Dickinson, Colchester, Ct., he was ordained at Paterson, N. J., June 28, 1854. In May 1, 1856, he was installed at Westminster, and was dismissed therefrom June 9, 1859. In 1859—'62 he served as acting pastor at North Chelsea, now Revere, and from 1862 to 1875 he was Superintendent and Chaplain of the Industrial school for girls in Lancaster. In the years 1875—'88 he supplied churches in Shirley, Orange and Lancaster. In 1879—86 he was Chaplain of State Institutions at Cranston, R. I. He then became acting pastor at Thompson, Ct., until his death at Pepperell, Dec. 11, 1887. He was married, Oct. 15, 1853 to Jane A. Vanderburgh, Syracuse, N. Y., and left two children, Dr. Herman V. Ames, now of the University of Pennsylvania, and a daughter, Ella E. Ames, of Philadelphia, one son having deceased.

Rev. Mr. Ames was especially interested in reform work. An obituary notice from the Providence *Journal* of Dec. 29, 1887, states that "he had a tender heart toward the criminal classes. While he abhorred the crimes they had committed, he was, nevertheless, a firm believer in the possibility of their reformation under the inspiration and power of the Gospel." It was his endeavor to make Reform schools truly reformatory rather than penal, and in those schools of which he had charge many wayward ones were inspired to lead a better life. He was also greatly interested in mission work, and was, indeed, in early life appointed missionary physician to the Gabboon Mission, Africa, but his wife's health proving inadequate, the plan had to be abandoned. Besides his annual Reports as Superintendent of the Schools, he was the author of several addresses on Temperance and Reform. In his theology, he was strongly Calvinistic, and as a preacher he was brilliant, fervent and impressive. In his drawing power as a man and speaker he may be called magnetic. His obituary closes with these words: "He was a broad man of strong sympathies, keen perceptions and indomitable will; pure minded and sweet-spirited, he lived to bless the world, and, dying, left a void that cannot readily be filled."

WILLIAM HENRY STETSON, of South Scituate, was born in Boston, Nov. 14, 1820, and died in Providence, March 13, 1897. After leaving the Academy and teaching school for a time, he took a four years' course in the Methodist Biblical Institute at Concord, N. H. He spent some 45 years in the Gospel ministry, serving parishes in the Norwich, New Bedford and Providence Districts, which were regarded as above the ordinary rank. In 1874—77 he was Presiding Elder of the Norwich District, and in 1877—79 of the New Bedford District. In Falmouth, the place of his first settlement, he was married on May 9, 1853, to Miss Lucy F. Nye, who with one son and three daughters survives him.

GEO. A. LITCHFIELD, a student of the Academy under Mr. Conant, afterward studied for two years at Brown University, leaving there in 1862, when the war broke out. He was settled over the Baptist Church in Winchendon five years when he resigned on account of ill-health and has never since taken a pastorate. When he, with his sister Ophelia, attended the Academy, his parents lived in this village, but while a student in College they resided, I think, in Brookfield. His present residence is Wollaston.

REV. D. P. HATCH.

DAVID P. HATCH was born in "the two-miles," Marshfield, Oct. 16, 1856. After studying at the Academy he took the course at Phillips Andover Academy, and subsequently graduated from Amherst College in 1883, and from Hartford Theological Seminary in 1886. He was ordained and installed in Rockland, Me., July 1, 1886, and remained there until May, 1895, and then took a three months' tour in Europe. On returning in the Fall of 1895, he was chosen Secretary of the Maine Missionary Society, which office he still holds.

His present address is Portland, Me. In Oct. 27, 1886, he married Miss Caroline, daughter of Professor Patton, of Washington, D. C., who died Jan. 19, 1893, and in Jan. 9, 1895 he was married again to Miss Cora E. Johnson, of Williamstown, Mass. His only child, born Dec. 11, 1895, lived but about two years.

(I would here speak a word as to the character and worth of Mr. Hatch's mother, who attended the Academy for awhile with myself. She was a ladylike, cultured Christian woman, a woman of talent, who could write poetry or could write sermons, which last, however, I was not permitted to see. In my estimation she was in every way a superior woman. I trust that among our

ANN S DWELLEY (HATCH).

numerous Alumnæ there is many an Almira Little (previously mentioned) and many an Ann S. Dwelley, who are the choice ones of earth and heaven, and whose names, though unrecorded on the printed page, yet deserve to be noticed quite as much as many that will be mentioned in this work.)

MR. JAMES C. CHURCH, of So. Scituate, after teaching some time in our public schools, studied in Canton, N. Y., to be a Universalist minister, and was first settled in Maine. Afterward he joined the Congregational denomination, but its year book no longer bears his name in the list of preachers. He is now engaged in business in Boston.

WILLIAM C. LITCHFIELD was born in So. Scituate, near "Studley Hill," March 31, 1840, and after attending the Academy in 1852—53 and 1856—57, prepared under private instruction to enter Meadville Theological Seminary in 1861. The Civil War breaking out, he sought to enlist in the 18th Mass. Regt., Co. G., but failed to pass examination. In 1864, however, he enlisted in Co. E., 1st Heavy Artillery, and served until the close of the war. During the years 1877—78 he served as Selectman, and in 1878—79 was Representative from the District embracing the towns of So. Scituate, Scit-

REV. WM. C. LITCHFIELD.

uate, and Cohasset. After reading Theology under direction of Prof. F. H. Hedge, of Cambridge, he was ordained at Hobart, Ind., in May, 1879, a minister of the Unitarian denomination. His settlements have been in Gardner, Berlin and Middleboro, in which latter place he now resides. In Sept., 1894, a severe illness rendered him unable longer to assume the duties of a settled pastor. In the recent State election Mr. Litchfield was chosen Republican Representative from Middleboro for 1899.

ERNEST A. THOMAS, of Marshfield has for some time been supplying the Baptist Church in Three Rivers, but I believe he has never been ordained. His present address is Roxbury District, Boston.

ALUMNI WHO, ACCORDING TO MY RECOLLECTION, HAVE GRADUATED FROM COLLEGES AND SEMINARIES.*

J. J. Ellis, D. B. Ford, F. O. Barstow, from Brown; Geo. M. Reed, C. L. Howes, D. P. Hatch, from Am-

*It is, of course, understood that all the College graduates mentioned did not receive their entire fitting at Hanover Academy, though many did so. Some certainly studied elsewhere, while they took their start from here.

herst, Geo. R. Dwelley, Franklin E. Felton, Edward G Stetson, from Harvard; C. Hitchcock, George A. Collamore, Leander Collamore, from Dartmouth; Harry T. Watkins from Colby; F. S. Thomas, from Harvard Medical School; W. P. Brooks, from Massachusetts Agricultural College; Frank Baker and Charles B. Phillips from West Point; J. W Beal from Institute of Technology; H. L. Sweeny, from Adams Academy; Wm. H. Stetson from Concord Methodist Biblical Institute; Edward Southworth, Emily E. Sylvester, Martha W. Sylvester, Grace F. Hatch, Grace L. Russell, from Bridgewater Normal School; Emma Barstow, Angela B. Ford, Edith G. Ford, from Wheaton Female Seminary; Florina M. Collamore from Thayer Academy.

As many of the above names have been noticed elsewhere, we shall only speak of two or three farther.

PROF. WILLIAM PENN BROOKS was born in So. Scituate, Nov. 19, 1851. At about the age of fourteen he attended the "Assinippi Institute," and on its closing he came to the Academy. After teaching in several of our Hanover schools and in Rockland, he entered the Massachusetts Agricultural College at Amherst, and graduated therefrom in 1875 with the degree of B. Sc.

PROF WM. PENN BROOKS

In the following year he was a post-graduate student in Chemistry, Botany and the Languages. In 1877—88 we find him professor of Agriculture in the Imperial College of Agriculture in Sapporo, Japan, and for several years he was acting President of that college. Since 1889 he has served as Professor of Agriculture at Amherst, and as Agriculturalist for the Hatch Experiment Station. One year, 1896—7, he spent in Europe, in travel and study, and in the latter year received the degree of Ph. D. from the University of Halle-Wittenberg, Germany. In March 28, 1882, he was married to Eva Bancroft Hall, and has two children, Rachel Bancroft, born Jan., 1884, and Sumner Cushing, born Aug., 1888.

FRANK BAKER, son of Geo. Martin Baker, of Marshfield, graduated at West Point in 1872, as No. 5 in a class of 57 members. Commissioned as 2d Lieut. 13th Regt. of Infantry, Instructor at the Military Academy and with Regiments in Wyoming, Louisiana, Mississippi and Georgia. First Lieut. 13th Infantry, Nov. 1, 1874. Transferred to Ordnance Dept of the Army as 1st Lieut., April, 18, 1879. Served at Arsenals in Rock Island, Ill., Benicia, Cal., Philadelphia, Pa., and Watertown, Mass. Capt. Ordnance Dept. 1886, and now Inspector of Ordnance U. S. A., at Providence, R. I. His brother GEORGE BAKER, has served for several years as one of the Selectmen of Marshfield, and was a member of the Legislature in 1882.

In Mr. J. WILLIAMS BEAL we recognize a skilled Architect, not imported from abroad, but born and bred among us. There was in his make-up as a boy a considerable amount of play, but any excessiveness of this quality he in due time suppressed, and with great persistency of purpose took a full course of technological instruction, and became thereby one of our most widely known, accomplished and successful Architects. In Hanover he will probably be best and longest remembered as the designer of its beautiful Soldiers' Monument. Mr. Beal early took to himself in life's partnership an Academy girl, Mary W. Howes, only daughter of our long beloved village physician, Dr. Woodbridge R. Howes, late deceased, and he is now blessed with a fine family of children.

Another Academy student who has likewise distinguished himself in the business of Architecture, Engineering, Surveying, Draughting, is WILLARD KENT, of Marshfield, who attended the Academy under Mr. Keene's instruction. He has now offices at Woonsocket and at Narragansett Pier, R. I.

GEO R DWELLEY.

GEORGE RUSSELL DWELLEY, after leaving the Academy, prepared for college at Andover, and graduated from Harvard University, class of 1853. After teaching a few years in the Rockland High School and many years in the High School at Watertown, he went West, and served three or four years as Bookkeeper for a Copper Mining Company at Lake Superior. Returning to Boston he became Treasurer of the Mechanics Savings Bank, and was also appointed as its receiver. He then took up his school work in Watertown, and has served as teacher or School Superintendent there over a score of years. His present address is Arlington Heights.

We reprint the following verses by Mr. Dwelley as we find them in a local sheet of recent date. The last lines, though true as a general thing, do not wholly do away with the regret which we feel at the Academy's demise:

A TRIBUTE TO THE HANOVER ACADEMY.

Suggested by the announcement that the Academy building was to be sold.

In the views of the fathers the schoolhouse came next
To food, clothing and shelter; church, parson and text.
And those schools were the best in their scale of esteem,
Which gave of sound knowledge the cream of the cream.
Hence academies flourished; and each little town
Had its Liliput college for jacket and gown,
Where the boy could his faculties freely unfold,
And the girl bud and bloom into beauty of soul;
And where guidance of masters made easy of reach
Both strength for the spirit and grace for the speech.

Our Hanover folk, in their guesses at truth,
Deemed the best none too good for their innocent youth.
So, with foresight of students to come by the score,
They built in their faith one academy more.
What a blessing it was! And what blessing it brought
To the many it raised to new levels of thought!
What friendships it fostered! They live till to-day
In that kingdom within us which knows not decay;
How its influence grew, as its graduates spread,
Making life more worth living, and death the less dread!

"Let by-gones be by-gones," may moralists preach,
But the lesson is heartless their sermon would teach;
For there's little at anchor. Time sweeps most away,
And change succeeds change like the scenes in a play.
Ere a century passed, as a wreck on the shore
Lay the school that we cherished—its usefulness o'er.
While we tenderly mourn for the "day that is dead,"
We rejoice that a brighter has dawned in its stead;
And, with love for what has been, as optimists feel
That the High School serves better the whole common weal.

It will not, I trust, be deemed invidious if I mention a few of our Alumni who have become distinguished as business men and as honored and useful citizens.

SAMUEL TOLMAN, JR.

SAMUEL TOLMAN, JR., Son of Col. Samuel Tolman, born in So. Scituate in 1820, was a student in the Academy with myself, and was, indeed, in some studies a classmate, especially in the languages. He and Francis Collamore, Daniel C. Otis and myself studied Virgil together under Mr. Holmes who kindly permitted us to get our lessons in an ante-room or lobby, where, by a division of labor— each one looking out in the dictionary the meaning of different words—we could thereby make much more rapid progress than when studying alone. So enthusiastic were we at times in our studies (?) that the teacher was occasionally obliged to repress our enthusiasm either by speaking to us or by having our door set open so that he could take a distant observation. Mr. Tolman at one time thought of going to college, and probably would have done so but for considerations of health. For many years he was a Selectman in his native town, also a member of the school committee, and an honored Representative in General Court. But he is perhaps best remembered now for "his active interest in whatever pertained to the welfare and comfort of the brave men who went forth from that town to suffer and die that the Union might be preserved." I may add that the above portrait of Mr. Tolman was paid for by the Sabbath school of the Congregational church at Hanover Corners, of which school he was for a long time the Superintendent. His death occurred Nov. 27, 1894. His younger brother, James T. Tolman, whom I also knew as an Academy student under Mr. Holmes, died Jan. 29, 1896.

Perhaps no one among us was ever more respected in life and lamented in death than MR. CALVIN T. PHILLIPS of So. Hanover. In character and action he was almost an ideal man and citizen. For a time he was a most valued member of our Public Library Committee.

CALVIN T. PHILLIPS.

The report of that committee in 1892, consisting of

Rev. Melvin S. Nash and Mrs. D. B. Ford, has this tribute to his worth: " Himself a large and thoughtful reader of our best books, and greatly interested in our current literature, as also in the history of the past, he naturally felt a deep interest in this Library, and when chosen on its committee he sought both as a matter of duty and of pleasure in every possible way to promote its interests. . . . As members of the Library Committee we feel that in his removal from us we have sustained a loss which is well nigh irreparable." He was born in Hanson, March 3, 1836, married on October 31, 1865, to Maria E. Josselyn, and died Jan. 15, 1892.

MORRILL A. PHILLIPS.

MR. MORRILL A. PHILLIPS, another of our Academy boys, born in Hanson, Feb. 27, 1844, and now one of our most enterprising, useful and honored citizens, has been chosen to fill his brother's place as one of the Library trustees. He is a leading member of the large tack manufacturing firm of Ezra Phillips and Sons, to which his deceased brother also belonged. Mr. Phillips married Sophia R. Simmons, formerly a teacher in our public schools, and now (in 1898) chosen on our school committee. From their family of student daughters, I suspect the interests of education in future years will not be allowed to suffer.

WILLIAM CARVER BATES.

Of WILLIAM CARVER BATES, of his great interest in the welfare of the Academy, and of some of his public addresses and labors, we have already made brief mention. He was born in Hanover, May 25, 1838, attended the Academy in 1852—54, married on April 14, 1863, an Academy pupil, Miss Emma Barstow, resides in Newton, of which city he is a prominent citizen, and of whose Council he has been a member, and is now engaged in mercantile business in Boston.

Mr. Bates is largely interested in historical research, and has written many papers for literary, historical and genealogical societies, and for clubs of divers names, and has been a frequent speaker in our patriotic and civic gatherings. He has several times visited the West Indies, and has shown much descriptive talent in his " Rambles in the Tropics," and in his account of " Venezuela and British Guiana."

Enlisted in the war, May 1, 1861, he was taken prisoner at Bull Run, July 21, and was ten months in rebel prisons, at Richmond, New Orleans, and Salisbury, N. C., an account of which was published in the New England Magazine for April, 1895. After regaining his freedom he edited and published a little work entitled "The Stars and Stripes in Rebellion," (now in our Public library) which consists of a series of papers written by Federal prisoners to while away the time while residing in different rebel prisons.

EUGENE H. CLAPP.

As a man of large business talent we may mention the name of EUGENE H. CLAPP, deceased, who was for about three years connected with the Academy. He was born in the adjoining town of S. Scituate, Oct. 11, 1843. He started the great rubber manufacturing plant in our village which now gives employment to a very large number of hands. He also was connected with many other business enterprises, and was moreover specially interested in the great cause of temperance, and remembered that cause in his will. I think he was head of the Sons of Temperance of the United States, and was more than once urged to become a prohibition candidate for high office in this State. A biographical sketch of him is given in the Temperance Record for Feb., 1889, and in the Plymouth County Biographical Review. He was twice married and has had several children. His brother, George A. Clapp, who now stands at the head of the manufacturing Co., though not an Academy Alumnus, yet took for his wife an Academy girl and school teacher, Abbie A. Stetson, of Pembroke, and now resides in So. Hanover.

FREDERIC W. CLAPP, of So. Scituate, a cousin of the above, was for some years a partner in the rubber business. After amassing great wealth by a ten years' residence abroad, he returned to the United States and bought an estate in Framingham where he lived until his death in 1879. He served for some time as Representative to General Court, from Framingham. In 1868 he married Mary A. Lewis, and has left several children.

FRANK A. CLAPP, a brother of Frederic, was born in So. Scituate, Nov. 5, 1839, married Juletta, daughter of Mr. Robert Sylvester, of this village, lives in Wakefield, and has two children. He was for two years, 1880 and 1881, a Representative from Boston.

LUTHER BRIGGS, son of Luther and Susanna (Stetson) Briggs, and brother of our poetess, Mrs. Cheney, was born in Pembroke, July 24, 1822. In 1832—33 he attended the excellent private School of Mrs. Charlotte S. Wade, before mentioned. During the summers of 1834—5—7, he studied at the Academy, then under the tuition of Mr. White. In the meantime he was pursuing his studies at Scituate Harbor under the direction of Mr.

LUTHER BRIGGS.

Washburn, a former Academy teacher, and subsequently also at Bridgewater, under the tuition of Hon. John A. Shaw, who at a later date became Superintendent of Schools in New Orleans, where he had Jefferson Davis as one of his pupils. One winter Mr. Briggs taught a public school in Duxbury. For two summers he was employed on Government works at Forts Warren and Independence in Boston Harbor. Soon afterward he commenced business as "Architect, Civil Engineer and Surveyor," and has had an office in Boston for more than fifty years. During this time he has designed many public and private buildings for this and foreign countries, and has also been engaged in laying out estates, surveying railroads, and in designing and erecting beacons in Boston Harbor and on the Massachusetts coast. In the spring of 1894 he visited England and most of the principal cities of Europe.

ADELINE BRIGGS.

In July 7, 1847, he was married to Adeline, daughter of Horace Collamore, Esq., (of whose helpful aid in my writing I have already made mention, and whose portrait I am happy here to present,) and on July 7, 1897, they celebrated their golden anniversary. They reside in Neponset, near Boston, and have no children. I wish to add in regard to Mrs. Briggs that in all her letters to me she invariably speaks well of her different teachers, and so I judge her to have been a model scholar, and I am sorry that I could not elsewhere give a picture of herself as an Academy pupil. Of her sister, Julia Collamore, who attended the Academy at the same time with myself, I have the most pleasant recollections. I think she passed away in comparatively early life.

HORACE COLLAMORE.

Horace Collamore, Esq., father of Adeline, Julia, Dr. Francis and Leander, already named, was son of Capt. Enoch Collamore, who marched to the Lexington alarm, and was born in Scituate, now Norwell, Nov. 4, 1791, the youngest of eight children who survived infancy. With a view to professional life he became a pupil of Hanover Academy under the instruction of Rev. Mr. Chaddock, studying the languages and higher mathematics. Diverted, however, from this purpose by divers circumstances, he engaged in 1812 in the crockery and glass business in Boston, in which business he continued nine years, till failing health compelled him to retire to the country. In Sept. 20, 1814, he married Laura Briggs of Pembroke, and they lived to celebrate their golden wedding. In 1821 he became a resident of Pembroke, and thenceforth devoted his time to farming, keeping a country store, etc. He was a member of the Plymouth County Agricultural Society from its start, its supervisor for several years, and one of its Vice Presidents. He wrote a good hand with a facile pen, and often contributed valuable articles to the leading agricultural journals of the day. He was Brigade Major and Inspector of the 1st Brigade, 5th Division of the Massachusetts Militia. For a considerable period he was Postmaster of Pembroke, and for several years was Justice of the Peace and of the Quorum. In 1841 and '42 he was Representative to the General Court, and in 1853 was chosen Senator from the Plymouth District. Eleven children were born to him, ten of whom, five sons and five daughters, lived to maturity, and all of them received their education in large part at Hanover Academy, in which Institution he took a deep interest, and of which he was for many years a Trustee. He died Aug. 27, 1867. The above photograph was taken when he was 73 years old.

HORACE L. COLLAMORE.

HORACE LORENZO COLLAMORE, eldest son of Horace Collamore, Esq., was born in Boston, Dec. 8, 1816, but removed with his parents to Pembroke in 1821. He attended the "Plymouth County Seminary," established by Mrs. Charlotte S. Wade, of whom we have previously spoken, and became a student of Hanover Academy under the tuition of Mr. Rolfe, Rev. Mr. Wolcott, and Dr. Ira Warren. Subsequently he attended the Bridgewater Academy under the instruction of the distinguished educator, John A. Shaw. In our Academy he had for his classmates Frederick Jacobs, John Curtis, the founder of our Free Library, William H. Whitman, clerk of Plymouth County Court, William Paley Allen, son of Rev. Morrill Allen, and his cousin, Andrew F. Collamore, of whose sad fate mention will be made on a subsequent page. After leaving school he spent a few years in Boston, and then took up his residence in Kingston, where he managed a country store, served as Postmaster, and held various town offices. In 1861 he returned to Boston, and engaged for some 19 years in the Auction and Commission business. He was a deep thinker and a well-read man, was quiet and unassuming in manner, and made friends wherever he went. He was a member of the Mt. Lebanon Lodge of Freemasons for more than thirty years, and was known as one of the few remaining, pronounced, Jacksonian Democrats of the old school. On the tariff and the finance he was regarded as an able authority, and in defence of his political principles he used both voice and pen until about the period of his death, which latter event occurred on June 9, 1897. In Jan. 31, 1843, he married Lydia, daughter of David and Lydia (Foster) Beal, of Kingston, and has left as survivors a daughter and two grandchildren.

ISAAC GILMAN STETSON, one of our Academy students, was the son of Isaac O. and Emily (Josselyn) Stetson, and was born Aug 7, 1826. In 1846 he married an Academy girl and school teacher, Jane Reed Oldham, who was born Oct. 31, 1825, and died April 2,

1892   Mr. Stetson died most suddenly Aug. 17, 1897, aged nearly 72 years. For 18 years he was a Selectman, Assessor and Overseer of the town of Hanover, and was serving in those offices at the time of his death. For many years he was a store keeper and Postmaster in So. Hanover, and in 1885 was elected to our State Legislature. He was highly esteemed as a neighbor, a citizen, a town officer, and an efficient business man, and was especially noted in all these positions for his great geniality of manner and spirit. His associates in office have borne public testimony to their "appreciation of his worth as an officer, his integrity as a citizen, and his agreeable companionship as a co-worker;" and the town has also placed on record its testimony to his high character, to his worth as a man and to the value of his labors as a faithful official. "A friend, genial and true, his pleasant face was a mirror, reflecting the emotions of a warm, sympathetic heart."

HON. JEDEDIAH DWELLEY

HON. JEDEDIAH DWELLEY, a younger brother of George R. Dwelley, was born in Hanover, Feb. 28, 1834, and studied for a time in the Academy under the administration of Mr. McLauthlin. When but twenty-five years of age he was chosen Selectman, and served in that capacity for thirty years. For some twelve years he was also a member of the School Committee. In 1865 he was chosen Representative to General Court, and in 1873 and '74 he served as Senator. For nine or ten years he was special County Commissioner, and is now (1898) serving his twenty-second year as County Commissioner, being in length of service the senior County Commissioner in the Commonwealth. He was Chairman of the Selectmen during the war (being the youngest chairman in the State), and has ever taken a deep interest in the welfare of the soldiers. And this same interest he has ever manifested in all that concerns the welfare of the town both by his official life and as a private citizen, and no one has better deserved to be honored as a father of the town than he. Speaking, however, of himself he says: "If it can be truthfully said that I have loved mercy and dealt justly, personally, this would seem to me greater honor than to recount my years of official service."

BENJAMIN BARSTOW TORREY, son of Capt. Haviland and Salome (Barstow) Torrey, was born in Pembroke, Nov. 22, 1837. He attended Hanover Academy when under the tuition of Messrs. McLauthlin and Conant, and also the "University Grammar School" of Providence, R. I. On August 25, 1858, he entered the

BENJAMIN BARSTOW TORREY.

service of the Boston and Providence Railroad Company, and since 1867 has been Treasurer of that Corporation. In 1864 he was elected a member of the " New England Historic, Genealogical Society " of Boston, and has been its Treasurer since 1870. Our readers will perchance remember that he was, by his uncle, John Barstow, made a Trustee of the fund which he gave to the Academy. In 1865 he was married to Abby Vose Bent of Milton, who died September, 1897, leaving no children. He now resides in Boston, and the well-known " Broad Oak " mansion, (see Barry's History, p. 227) built by his grandfather, Col. John B. Barstow, but since owned and for a time occupied by himself, now stands empty. I trust the time will come when he will again become its occupant.

LEMUEL C. WATERMAN.

LEMUEL CUSHING WATERMAN was for many years a director and clerk of the Hanover Academy Corporation. In examining its Records I have always found it a pleasure to look at and to read his neat, plain, beautiful handwriting. He was born in So. Scituate, near Church Hill, July 14, 1814, and finished his education in the Academy in his eighteenth year. After a short term of business in Boston his health failed, and thereafter for several years he engaged in school keeping in places not far from home. Subsequently he was employed in the tack and nail factory of Mr. Samuel Salmond on the third herring brook, and finally attained the position of Superintendent of the works. Afterward he commenced the manufacture of tacks and nails at Project Dale, Hanover. In his later years he had the care and settlement of the large estate left by George Curtis. For many years he was a Selectman and a member of the School Committee of his native town, and in 1858 he represented the towns of So. Scituate and Hanover in the Legislature. His death occurred in March 11, 1889.

RUDOLPHUS C. WATERMAN.

RUDOLPHUS C. WATERMAN, eldest son of Lemuel C. and Elizabeth B. (Gooding) Waterman, was born in So. Scituate, June 16, 1840, and attended school at the Academy under the tuition of Frederic O. Barstow and Charles A. Reed. In 1858 he went to Boston and was there engaged in the wholesale drug and paint business with Messrs. Bird & Co. until 1862 when he enlisted for the war in the 44th Mass. Vols. After his return, he engaged in the tack manufacturing business of his father, which is now carried on at Project Dale, Hanover, by himself and members of his family. In 1866 he took for his wife M. Adele

Tomlinson of Boston, who died Jan. 27, 1895, aged 52 years, leaving two sons, William R. and Harry Cushing Waterman,—an only daughter, Lillian Adele, aged six years, having died previously. In 1880 he served as Selectman of Hanover, and in 1882 was a member of the Legislature. For many years Mr. Waterman has been a director of the Academy, and has succeeded to his father as Clerk of the Corporation. Mr. W. is rightly numbered as one of our most worthy and honored citizens.

Mr. EDMUND Q. SYLVESTER, eldest son of Mr. Michael Sylvester, was for many years either a Treasurer or a Director of Hanover Academy. When in an earlier page of my *first* manuscript I wrote of the forty-three original stockholders of the present Academic property, his name was mentioned as one of the then surviving five, but this name must now be put in the list of the starred. His death occurred on Sunday morning, April 17, 1898. He married for his first wife, Mary, and for his second wife, Eliza S., daughters of Samuel Salmond, and he leaves, besides the widow, five sons and one daughter, the wife of Rev. F. S. Harraden, to mourn his loss.* A man of large business enterprise, he for many years carried on the tack business at the Tiffany factory under the firm name of Samuel Salmond & Son, while at the same time he cultivated a large farm at

---

*While these pages were passing through the press, the youngest son, Francis Baldwin Sylvester, was taken from earth after a brief illness, March 2, 1899.

I may here add that only a few days after this, March 28, "my venerable neighbor friend," (referred to in the Preface), Mr. Robert Sylvester, uncle to the above Mr. Edmund, likewise passed away at the age of 93 years, 5 months. This leaves only two surviving grantees, Martin P. McLauthlin of Malden and Robert E. Dwelley of Hanover.

home. His beautified homestead estate, on the east side of Washington street, a part of which was once a rocky pasture, bears witness to his enterprise and his taste for the beautiful. He was a man of great wealth, yet liberal withal, and he seldom refused to help a needy applicant who was known to be worthy.

G. F. STETSON.

GEORGE F. STETSON, of Hanson, born April 11, 1833, served many years on the School Committee of Hanson, a part of the time as Chairman, was for six years, through and after the Civil War, U. S. Assistant Assessor of Internal Revenue for the towns of Hanson, and Hanover, was Representative for Hanson, Halifax and Plympton in 1861 and '62, also for Hanson, Pembroke, Halifax and Marshfield in 1879 and 1883. In the Legislature he took a very active part in favor of prohibitory legislation. In 1879 he made a minority report from the liquor committee, proposing the substitution of prohibition for license, and sustained the same in a speech which was complimented on the spot by no less a man than Judge Russell. At the close of that session, Gov. Talbot presented him with the pen with which he signed the Civil Damage (temperance) Bill. In 1883, as House Chairman of the Joint Standing Committee on the Liquor Law he presented and advocated in the House a proposition for Constitutional Prohibition, the first speech of that kind which was ever made in the Massachusetts Legislature. Judging from his official action in the cause of temperance, one may properly conclude that he never applied "hot and rebellious liquors in his blood," either in youth or age, even as he would forbid to others any like application.

MRS STETSON.

Mr. Stetson, on December 3, 1861, took for his wife an Academy girl, Dorothy Brown Dyer, daughter of Hervey and Ruth (Reed) Dyer. She was born March 29, 1835, and died June 2, 1884, leaving two children, Florence D. (Josselyn) born April 26, 1874, and George H., born April 14, 1878. "She was a most capable, diligent and successful teacher, teaching almost constantly in Pembroke and Hanson from the time she left the Academy until her marriage. Though declining to accept the position, she was the first female elected to serve upon the School Committee of Hanson." As I was wholly unacquainted with this devoted and faithful teacher, it gives me great pleasure to have seen her portrait and to have it printed, and I trust that many others will be equally pleased. Both parties were about thirty-five years of age when their pictures were taken.

We are glad to record the fact that MR. JOHN CURTIS who founded our HANOVER FREE LIBRARY, and recently

gave to the town $4000 as a Library Fund, and hopes
to do still more for that cause in the future, was an Academy student. He was born in No. Hanover, on Curtis
street, July 10, 1817 (not 1816 as in Barry), and in early
life attended the common schools for a few months in winter. The teachers, who were mainly from the vicinity,
had but a smattering of education, and generally re-

MR. JOHN CURTIS.

sumed their customary employments when the school
term was over. Lessons were learned and recited by
rote from the text books, and unaccompanied with any
explanation. Fortunately the school was taught one
winter by a student, afterwards a teacher, of the Wesleyan Academy of Wilbraham, who was a good scholar
and in sympathy with progress, but who was withal very

unpopular in the "deestrict." By him the parents of Mr. Curtis were persuaded to let their son go to Wilbraham for one year. On returning from the Wesleyan Academy he attended our Hanover Academy in 1833—4 under the tuition of Mr. Washburn and Ira Warren.*

While attending school here he, according to the custom of those days, was obliged to walk both ways, taking his noon lunch with him. "To revive my memory," he says, " I have been over the same route on foot when nearly an octogenarian—thanks to sound health." Upon leaving the Academy he went to Boston alone to find

---

*Mr. Curtis writes me that his most intimate friend in the Academy and subsequently in Boston, was Andrew Fuller Collamore, son of Deacon John Collamore, of Assinippi, to whom we have previously made reference. His tragic end on the steamer Atlantic, Nov. 25, 1846, is thus noticed in a certain publication lately received: "Mr. Andrew Collamore, a young business man of this city, who was widely known and esteemed in business and social circles, was journeying to New York to be married on Thanksgiving evening. On that fearful night the cold, icy waves of Long Island Sound embraced the ardent lover, and shrouded in grief the life of a beautiful and devoted young lady."

This new and elegant steamer struck on a reef of rock a few miles out from New London, in a fearful gale and snow storm, and was totally lost with upward of fifty passengers. This sad wreck, and the still sadder burning of the steamer Lexington on the same Long Island Sound on Jan. 13, 1840, when one hundred and fifty-six persons, many of them of great eminence, were burned or drowned, can never be forgotten by our people

To the above paragraphs I must now add the fearful loss which has just taken place (Nov. 27, 1898), of probably over 170 persons, constituting the entire company of the passengers and crew of the steamer Portland, which was driven on the shore of Cape Cod by the most terrific blizzard that was ever known in these parts, and by which, indeed, a large portion of our New England coast has been visited with wreckage, desolation and death. Let us be thankful for the assurance of prophecy that THERE SHALL BE NO MORE SEA.

some sort of position. With very flattering certificates of his character and abilities from Rev. Mr. Dunbar, of the No. Hanover Baptist church, and from his Wilbraham teacher, he obtained a situation with a clothing and tailoring firm, agreeing to stay with them until twenty-one years of age for $50 a year and his board. The contract was faithfully kept, and in consequence the firm helped him to set up in the clothing business for himself in his twenty-first year; and he continued in that business on the same spot, 6 and 8 North street, for nearly forty years, and then relinquished it to his nephew, Walter C. Brooks, another Hanover boy, now at 15 Milk street, which is Mr. Curtis' P. O. address.

Mr. Curtis' father early took Mr. Garrison's paper, "*The Liberator*, and Mr. C. was always deeply interested in the anti-slavery question. "About ten years ago I was invited," he says, "to attend a 'materializing seance' of the Spiritualists, and was so convinced of its stupendous fraud, I became interested in exposing the swindle. The result was that I published a pamphlet," etc. This, I think, was entitled "Some Account of the VAMPIRES OF ONSET, Past and Present." He says: "All that happened in Boston I know to be true, for I was in it as a leading actor."

Mr. Curtis has one artist daughter, Alice M., who has been recently travelling in Europe.

In addition to the full-page portrait of Mr. Curtis I desired a smaller picture taken in his earlier years, the choice of course being left to himself and family. The one presented above, taken from an old-fashioned miniature, was selected, probably, from an artistic point of view. Personally I should have preferred a portrait from a photograph in my possession which looks more as I used to know him when a business man.

HON. STEPHEN N. GIFFORD.

The most honored name, perhaps, that has ever been connected with Hanover Academy is that of HON. STEPHEN NYE GIFFORD. He was born in Pembroke, July 21, 1815, and died at his home in Duxbury, April 18, 1886. He was left fatherless at the early age of ten, the family were in humble and straitened circumstances, and he in his early youth engaged in shoemaking in the house now occupied by Conductor Charles E. Collamore, in Brickkiln street, No. Pembroke. I have been told that a neighbor friend of his, Susan S. (Briggs) Smith, greatly interested herself in the boy's welfare, and encouraged him to attend the Academy; and in this way, through many difficulties, he started on a long career of eminent usefulness and honor. After studying for a time in Bridgewater—paying his way by working at his trade out of school hours—he began teaching in the common schools (one term or more in Centre Hanover), and after some years established a private school in Duxbury. In 1850 he was chosen Representative, and the next year he was appointed inspector in the Boston Custom House. After serving for brief periods as State Auditor and as Assistant Clerk in the Senate and House, he in 1858 was chosen Clerk of the Senate, and held this office nearly twenty-nine years, until the time of his death, a continuance in that office which is unparalleled in the history of the Commonwealth. In 1882, March 10, after twenty-four years of this service, a "Complimentary Dinner" was given to him by the Senate in the United States Hotel, Boston, "in honor of the faithful service of a true man who for many years has adorned the trust reposed in him, by every quality which should distinguish the public service, and by every grace of character which can attach him to his associates." His printed Memorial speaks of him as "A modest, unassuming, genial, kindly gentleman," who for "more than twenty-eight years has stood at his post of duty, the manly, the faithful, the dignified, the kind-hearted, aye, the big-hearted Clerk of the Massachusetts Senate." The amount of clerical labor which he performed, and of assistance which he unassumingly rendered in successive years to new Senators and to new Speakers cannot easily be described or conceived.

It seems altogether congruous that in connection with the preceding account of Mr. Gifford I should here give some notice of his early patroness and benefactor to whom he, at about the time the complimentary dinner was given him, wrote these words: "You especially were the first one who encouraged me to think that I was anything." Susan Stetson Briggs, eldest daughter of Luther and Susan (Stetson) Briggs, and sister of Luther Briggs, and Augusta (Briggs) Cheney, already named, was born July 26, 1813. She was a pupil of Mr. Holmes in the district school of No. Pembroke, and began her studies at the Academy under Mr. Rolfe. In April 5,

MRS. SMITH.

1838, she was married by Rev. Morrill Allen to Nathaniel Smith, grandson of Rev. Thomas Smith, the second minister of Pembroke, and on April 5, 1888 they celebrated their golden wedding. They had two children, Susan Augusta Smith, for a time an assistant teacher at the Academy, and Moses Bass Smith. He studied at the Academy, and was a youth of great promise, but lost his life April 5, 1861, in a shipwreck off Hatteras Inlet. Mr. Nathaniel Smith died March 25, 1890. The widow and daughter still reside in the pleasant old family homestead.

Alumni who have Taught School.

It is impossible for any one, unless possessed of omniscience, to give all the names of our Academy students (and there is quite a host of them) who have become teachers. I have however sought, at the request of some, to furnish a list of our Alumni and Alumnæ who have, chiefly within my own recollection, taught in our public schools and higher seminaries. Of course it is understood that other Academy students who have never taught may be quite the equals in talent and scholarship of those who did teach. Some of this latter class, indeed, only taught in the lower schools and but for a short time.

I am painfully aware that this list and other lists which precede and follow are very imperfect, containing some names which should be omitted, and omitting many names which should be inserted. If my friends will kindly send me any additions or corrections to any of these lists, I will see that they are inserted in a page of *Addenda et Corrigenda* in some future copies of this work.

Names of Male Teachers—William P. Allen, Stephen N. Gifford, Luther Briggs, Lemuel C. Waterman, Geo. R. Dwelley, Joshua J. Ellis, Francis Collamore, Leander Collamore, Geo. A. Collamore, Andrew T. Magoun, Charles Hitchcock, William H. Stetson, Geo. M. Reed, David A. Josselyn, Benjamin B. Torrey, Franklin Jacobs, William P. Duncan, John S. Crosby, Frederic O.

HISTORY OF HANOVER ACADEMY. 199

Barstow, Calvin T. Phillips, Clarence L. Howes, John P. Thorndyke, William P. Brooks, Charles B. Phillips, Joseph T. Corlew, Edward Southworth, Daniel K. Stetson, Samuel S. Knapp, James C. Church, Harry T. Watkins.

Names of Female Teachers—Nancy W. Collamore (Mitchell), Lavina A. Hatch, Mary B. Oldham (Perry), Jane R. Oldham (Stetson), Aurelia Hall (Bonney), Ann S. Dwelley (Hatch), Susan Magoun (Sherman), Adeline Collamore (Briggs), Augusta Briggs (Cheney), Lydia W. Collamore (Richardson), Lucinda Hatch (Oakman), Julia Collamore (Stodder), Sophia Clark (Holmes), Addie M. Stockbridge (Potter), Elizabeth A. Stockbridge (Allen), L. Elmina Curtis (Jacobs), Laura J. Duncan (King), Lucia A. Duncan (Dean), Amelia A. Stockbridge (Gardner), Sophia A. Holmes (Hatch), Lucy E. Boynton (Cromack), Mary A. Oldham, Mary Clark, Priscilla Clark (Eells), Emma Barstow (Bates), Hannah E. Brooks (Oakman), Lucy Vinal (Stetson), Mary Collamore (Ford), Sarah Collamore (Hitchcock), Helena M. T. Eells (Howland), Caroline D. Collamore (Loving), Arabella Collamore (Perrow), Sarah Hitchcock, Louisa Clark (Alden), Susanna F. Sylvester (Lapham), Juletta Sylvester (Clapp), Sarah E. Sylvester (Allen), Lydia Sylvester (Fuller), Huldah D. Freeman (Thrasher), Mary D. A. Hatch (Simonds), Susan P. Hatch (Perkins), Lucy A. Barstow (Waterman), Elizabeth T. Waterman (Sylvester), Clara H. Mann (Bonney), Laura F. Mann (White), Florina Mann, Helen M. Josselyn (Howland), Mary E. Barstow, Etta H. Barstow, Tryphena Whiting, Cynthia Whiting (Whiting), Sophia B. Loring (Taylor), Betsy H. Whiting (Whiting), Ellen

C. Gardner (Church), Mary L. Eells, Huldah B. Dwelley, Esther S. Magoun (Hazeltine), Nancy T. Magoun (Beale), Anna Tolman, Fidelia L. Howland (Barker), Mary P. Howland, Abby C. Donnell, Nancy C. Donnell, Rebecca J. Joyce (Josselyn), Polly B. Talbot (Knapp), Charlotte S. Gardner (Briggs), Ruth W. Stetson (Damon), Bessie H. Stetson (Josselyn), Susan J. Turner (Phinney), Addie W. Turner (Nash), Eliza M. Church (Billings), Lucy H. Chamberlain (Turner), Ophelia Litchfield (Rice), Florence V. Rogers (French), Ruthetta M. Sylvester, Emily E. Sylvester, Martha W. Sylvester (Turner), Angela B. Ford (Brock), Helen P. Barker (Chamberlain), Lydia W. Collamore (Sampson), Abbie C. Hatch, Ella J. Thomas (Paine), Abbie A. Stetson (Clapp), Eunice P. Simmons, Emma L. Stoddard (Packard), Hannah B. Hart (Pratt), Francis Turner (Harlow), Charlotte E. Winslow (Barnard), Ruth Magoun (Magoun), Susan M. Magoun (Chamberlain,) Lizzie Paulding, Anna P. Alden (Kingman), Grace L. Russell, Grace F. Hatch (Dana), Susan D. Stone, Elizabeth G. Stone, Harriet L. Garratt, Harriet P. Leach (Waterhouse), Dorothy B. Dyer (Stetson), Priscie C. Eells, Wealthy M. Magoun (Hall), Laura Barker (Little), Caroline T. Southworth (Prouty), Mary C. Tolman (Sheldon), Agnes Sherman, Alberta White (Hewson), Maria W. Tolman, Emma H. Torrey (Bates), Henrietta Collamore, Nellie D. Collamore, Mary E. Clapp, Anna M. Pratt (Upham), Mary E. Curtis, Bertha L. Buttrick (Whiting), Jennie M. Currell (Coleman), Mary A. Hunt, Annie N. Little.

Of those who have taught the longest we recall the following names: Mary E. Barstow, Mary L. Eells, the Whiting Sisters, Mary P. Howland, Anna Tolman, Edward Southworth.

SOMETHING FURTHER RESPECTING THE ALUMNI FUND.

On pages 122—124, some account is given of the raising and disposition of the Alumni Fund, and the statement was there made that the small balance remaining in the hands of the Trustees would probably be given to the Town for the Public Library. Accordingly the said Trustees have since conveyed to the town of Hanover the sum of $270 as a permanent fund for said Library, with the understanding that the income of said Fund should be used only for the purchase of books of permanent value (avoiding ephemeral works of light fiction) and that all books purchased from said fund should be thus inscribed :

" Purchased from the income of the Hanover Academy Alumni Fund, conveyed to the Trustees of the Hanover Free Library, April 1, 1899, by the Trustees of said Fund, William Carver Bates and David B. Ford."

There has recently been placed in my hands a list of those who subscribed to the Alumni Fund. I have already mentioned two persons, Rev. Samuel Cutler and Mrs. Albert Smith, who gave $100 each. Others who gave $100 apiece are :

George Curtis, Eliza Salmond, Joseph Smith, and Edmund Q. Sylvester. James R. Smith of New York city gave $50 ; William Carver Bates, Benjamin B. Torrey, Herbert Torrey, Isaac M. Wilder, Martin P. McLauthlin, Mrs. Gardner, Eugene H. Clapp, Lemuel C. Waterman, Rudolphus C. Waterman, and Mrs. Horatio Bigelow, gave $10 each ; Isaac Wilder, Robert Barstow, Morrill A. Phillips, Mrs. Farnham, Sarah E. Cushing, Irenæus L. Waterman, and George Briggs gave $5 each ; Benjamin Barstow and Warren I. Wright gave $3 each, and Mary Barstow $1.25. It will be noticed that of the first six donors above mentioned, who gave the largest sums, only one, E. Q. Sylvester, was an Academy Alumnus, and that all are now deceased. It is probable that, of the Alumni proper who gave to the Fund, only about half are now living. We may properly state that the movement for this fund was inaugurated (not in 1860, as the types have it on page 122, but in 1869), and carried on to a successful issue largely through the efforts of William Carver Bates.

Our Fallen Heroes.

"The muffled drum's sad roll has beat
The soldiers' last tattoo;
No more on life's parade shall meet
That brave and fallen few."

Died in the Service.

JOSEPH EELLS WILDER, of Hanover enlisted* in Co. D., 31st Regt. Infantry, Nov. 20, 1861, while a student in Amherst College, class of 1863. He served three

---

*Enlisted, as used in these notices, means generally the same as enrolled or mustered in. The dates I have taken mainly from the "Records of the Massachusetts Volunteers," Vols. 1, 11. It will be seen that a large proportion of our students enlisted in what may be termed the "Old Colony Regiment," the 18th, made up largely by enlistments from Plymouth County. This justly famed Regiment "shared in the battles on the Peninsula, and was engaged at the second Bull Run, Shepherdstown, Fredericksburg, Chancellorsville, Gettysburg, Rappahannock Station, Wilderness, Spottsylvania, Cold Harbor, Petersburg, and Weldon Rail Road. The casualties were numerous, and the regiment suffered severely—the killed and wounded numbering nearly two hundred and fifty." The historian says that to Hanover, among other towns, "is due the origin of this notably excellent Regiment."

years and re-enlisted Quarter Master Sergeant, February 11, 1864, and was killed while in charge of wagon train on the Red River Expedition under Gen. Banks, at Sabine Cross Roads, La., April 8, 1864, aged 25 years. In laying aside his cherished studies and professional aims at his country's call, few men have made a greater sacrifice than he. It is from him that the Post No. 83 G. A. R. of Hanover is worthily named,

JOSEPH EELLS WILDER.

and it is at the expense of this Post that the above picture is inserted.

"Wilder in his unknown grave sleeps well—fallen nobly, fighting for his country's cause. Ne'er beat a nobler heart, none had a truer friend—his was a glorious death, the brave, noble heart is still—beneath the cypress he sleeps, the murmur of the Red River his only requiem."—Tribute of C. C. Holmes, Newberne, 1876.

Loammi B. Sylvester, of Hanover, enlisted for three years, Feb. 27, 1862, in Reg. 2, Inf. Co. I., was wounded in the battle of Cedar Mountain, Va., Aug 9, 1862, and died in Alexandria, Sept. 7, 1862, aged 31 years.

Benjamin Curtis, of Hanover, enlisted August 6, 1862, in 12th Regiment, Company G, and was killed at Antietam, Md., September 17, 1862, aged 22 years. "A thoughtful young man, independent, impulsive and honest, a good scholar and a true friend."—Hon. Jedediah Dwelley.

Henry Currell, of Scituate, enlisted August 14, 1862, in 39th Infantry, Company C, and died in Andersonville Prison, Georgia, September 14, 1864.*

Nathaniel Walter Winslow, of S. Scituate, aged 22 years, enlisted August 5, 1862, in Regiment 18, Company G, and was killed in Shepardstown, Va., September 20, 1862, while swimming across a river.

William C. Oakman, of Marshfield, aged 31, enlisted August 19, 1862, in Regiment 35, Company C, and died on exchange boat October 6, 1864, of wounds received in Poplar Spring Church, Va., September 30, 1864.

Josiah Stoddard, Jr., of So. Scituate, aged 23, enlisted from Marshfield August 20, 1862, and died in Stuart's Hospital, Baltimore, November 19, 1862.

Calvin S. Magoun, of Pembroke, born November 14, 1839; enlisted October 9, 1861, in Regiment 23, Com-

---

* Of those from Plymouth County who joined this regiment a large proportion were from the towns of Hingham, Scituate and S. Scituate. The last year of its history was marked by heavy losses in killed, wounded and prisoners. The 39th was present at the surrender of Gen. Lee at Appomatox, Sunday, April 9, 1865.

pany A. Discharged for disability June 1, 1862. He was in the Burnside's Expedition and was at the taking of Roanoke Island and of Newbern, where he was taken sick. After spending some time in the hospital he was given a furlough and sought to return home, but died June 19, 1862, of typhoid pneumonia, in the cars on the Norwich train, between New York and Boston.

> "On Fame's eternal camping ground
> Their silent tents are spread,
> And Glory guards with solemn round
> The bivouac of the dead."

OTHER OF OUR ENLISTED ALUMNI.

JOSEPH F. STETSON, of Hanover, aged 21, enlisted in Regt. 18, Co. G., Aug. 24, 1861, re-enlisted Jan. 1, 1864, Regt. 32, Co. M. Sergt.

GEORGE F. STETSON, of So. Scituate, aged 25, enlisted Aug. 5, 1861, Regt. 18, Co. G., re-enlisted Jan. 2, 1864, transferred Oct. 26, 1864, to 32d Inf. Co. L. Corp.

EDWARD SOUTHWORTH, of So. Scituate, aged 24, enlisted July 31, 1862, Regt. 18th, Co. G., discharged Sept. 21, 1863, order War Department to receive an appointment as Second Lieutenant in the 2d Regt, U. S. colored troops. Promoted to First Lieut. Oct 6, 1864, and to Regimental Quartermaster, April 14, 1865, was honorably discharged Aug., 1865, on account of injuries received while in the service. He was in the battles of Antietam, Sharpsburg, Fredericksburg, Chancellorsville and Gettysburg.

GEORGE H. CLAPP, of So. Scituate, aged 21, enlisted in Regt. 18th Co. G., July 31, 1862, re-enlisted Feb. 9, 1864, transferred Oct. 26, 1864, to 32d Inf. Co. C.

CHARLES TOLMAN, of So. Scituate, aged 19, enlisted Regt. 18th, Co. G., Aug. 5, 1862, discharged Jan. 10, 1863, through disability.

LEBBEUS STOCKBRIDGE, of Hanover, aged 35, enlisted in Regt. 2d, Co. K., May 25, 1861 ; promoted Sergeant Major, Nov. 1, 1862.

GEORGE C. DWELLEY, of Hanover, aged 22, enlisted in Regt. 4th, Co. I., May 22, 1861, for three months, re-enlisted Aug. 2, 1862, in Regt. 12th, Co. G., for three years. Transferred Sept 1, 1863 to V. R. C. (Veteran Reserve Corps.)

WILLIAM H. BATES, of Hanover, aged 25, enlisted Aug. 20, 1862, Regt. 38th, Co. K., Corp. Discharged July 9, 1863, for disability.

MELZAR C. BAILEY, of Hanover, aged 23, enlisted 3d Regt. of Cavalry, Co. D., Sept. 6, 1862, re-enlisted Aug. 9, 1864, 1st Battalion Heavy Artillery, Co. E.

CYRUS C. HOLMES, of Hanover, aged 24, enlisted Regt. 18th, Co. G., Aug. 24, 1861, Sergt. Discharged Oct. 23, 1863, for disability, having been wounded in second battle of Bull Run.

ROBERT S. CHURCH, of Hanover, aged 20, enlisted for 9 months, Sept. 12, 1862, Regt. 43d, Co. G. Elected Capt. Military Co., District No. 62, Jan. 16, 1865.

WILLIAM CARVER BATES, aged 22, enlisted May 1, 1861, for three months, Regt. 5. Co. G., taken prisoner July 21, 1861, exchanged 1862.

THOMAS B. HOLMES, aged 17, enlisted Sept 21, 1861, in Regt. 24th, Co. E., musician.

THOMAS D. BROOKS, of Hanover, aged 21, enlisted Aug. 10, 1864, 1st Batt. Heavy Artillery, Co. E.

GEORGE B. OLDHAM, of Hanover, aged 23, enlisted August 20, 1862, in Regiment 38, Company K; promoted Sergeant, February, 1864.

OREN T. WHITING, of Hanover, aged 28, enlisted September 23, 1862, in Regiment 3, Company A, for three months. Re-enlisted for three years August 9, 1864, in 1st Battery, Heavy Artillery, Company E. Corp.

NATHANIEL CUSHING of Hanover, aged 18, enlisted February 1, 1864, 4th Regiment of Cavalry, Company K.

GEORGE W. WHITING, of Pembroke, aged 22, enlisted September 2, 1862, in Regiment 39, Company G; discharged for disability February 8, 1864.

FRANK T. WHITING, of Pembroke, aged 21, enlisted September 2, 1862, in Regiment 39, Company G.

WILLIAM C. LITCHFIELD, of So. Scituate, aged 24, enlisted August 10, 1864, 1st Battalion, Heavy Artillery, Company E.

AUGUSTUS JACOBS, of So. Scituate, aged 21, enlisted September 12, 1862, Regiment 44, Company D, for nine months.

ELISHA W. LAPHAM, of So. Scituate, aged 18, enlisted Aug. 24, 1861, Regt. 18, Co. G. Discharged for disability Oct. 25, 1862.

ABNER L. STETSON, of So. Scituate, aged 18, enlisted Aug. 4, 1862, Regt. 18th, Co. G., discharged for disability, March 9, 1863.

ALBERT W. CURTIS, of Pembroke, aged 21, enlisted Aug 24, 1861, Regt. 18th, Co. G., re-enlisted Jan. 2, 1864, Corp. Transferred Oct. 26, 1864, to Regt. 32d, Infantry, Co. I.

JOHN F. HATCH, of Marshfield, aged 18, enlisted Sept. 12, 1862, Regt. 43d, Co. F., for 9 months.

EDWARD R. CHURCH, of Pembroke, aged 25, enlisted Sept. 23, 1862, in Regt. 4th, Co. I, for 3 months, Corp. (This company saw very hard service in Louisiana.)

ELISHA F. COLEMAN, of So. Scituate, aged 19, enlisted Nov. 14, 1861, in Regt. 32, Co. A. Discharged March 2, 1863, for disability.

JUDSON EWELL, of Marshfield, enlisted Jan. 27, 1862, in Co. G. Second District of Columbia Volunteers. He was in the battle of Antietam, and was promoted to the rank of Sergeant.

RUDOLPH C. WATERMAN, of Scituate, aged 22, enlisted Sept. 12, 1862, in Regt. 44, Co. D., for 9 months, Corp.

HORACE S. TOWER, of Hanover, aged 18, enlisted Feb. 18, 1864, in 4th Regt. of Cavalry, Co. L. Corp.

JAMES L. HUNT, aged 33, enlisted Regt. 35, Co. H, Aug. 19, 1862. Discharged May 11, 1865, for disability.

CHARLES B. PHILLIPS, of Marshfield, a graduate at West Point, saw some service in the field.

GEORGE BAKER, of Marshfield, aged 30, enlisted March 30, 1863, Regt. 54, Co. C.

FRANK BAKER, whom we have previously noticed, served with his Regiment, (the 13th Infantry) in various parts of the United States. In 1879 he was transferred to the Ordnance Department of the army.

FREDERICK W. CLAPP, in service from Sept., 1862 until July, 1863, Regt. 43d, Co. G.

JOHN CORTHELL, enlisted Aug. 7, 1862, Regt. 39th, Co. G., and was discharged at the end of the war, June 8, 1865.

GEORGE H. SAMPSON was high private, U. S. Vols.

EDWIN J. CHANDLER, enlisted 1862—63, I think, from Duxbury.

GEORGE A. COLLAMORE, M. D., served in the war as surgeon of 100th Regt., Ohio Volunteers.

ENTERED THE NAVY.

Haviland Barstow, Gustavus Percival, Robert S. Talbot, Zephaniah Talbot, Henry H. Collamore, Robert E. Barstow, Edward P. Stetson.*

The following poetical tribute to the Soldiers and Sailors who enlisted and who fell in the war for the preservation of the Union was written by Mrs. Rev. Cyrus W. Allen for the Grand Army Fair, October 16—18, 1877, which was held to procure the Soldiers' Monument in Hanover. We subjoin it here because in the main it is appropriate to this section of our work, and because we deem it worthy to be placed on permanent historic record.

---

*Some acount of Haviland Barstow is given by William C. Bates in the Soldiers' Memorial. Henry H. Collamore was in the Navy from January 10, 1863 to Sept 19, 1865, at first as Acting Master's Mate, the last year as Acting Ensign.

HISTORY OF HANOVER ACADEMY.

MRS. C. W. ALLEN.

Hark! heard ye not the thunder loud,
  Echo along our southern shore?
Saw ye the lightning in the cloud?
  Heard ye the sullen ocean's roar?

Surely a tempest must be near!
  Seek shelter from the coming storm;
God keep your wives and children dear,
  Secure amid the dread alarm!

But look! the *sky* is clear and bright,
  The gentle breezes softly blow;
No cloud obscures the sun's fair light,
  All nature smiles beneath its glow.

What *means* this rumbling from afar?
  What trouble does this noise portend?
It means the approach of civil war
  Where men with brother men contend.

From East to West, from North to South,
  The electric wire the news conveys;
The message goes from mouth to mouth—
  "Fort Sumter's taken! rouse ye braves!"

Could we sit tamely by, and see
    The flag our fathers gave in trust
To proudly wave o'er land and sea
    Lie low and trailing in the dust?

Could we sit by and see the States,
    United once, asunder torn?
The chains that bound our fellow men
    Made still more grievous to be borne?

For months the South had been employed
    Arming themselves to meet this hour;
And aided by the rebel Floyd
    Were ready to assert their power.

In vain our Lincoln, good and wise,
    The folly of their course exposed;
In vain all terms of compromise,
    In Congress, Crittenden proposed.

"Let us alone," their leaders cried,
    "We'll stand alone," they loudly boast;
And added with a scornful pride
    "We'll take your forts upon our coast."

Then burst upon our startled ear
    The booming cannon's loud report;
On every side the guns we hear
    Firing against the fated fort.

The little famished loyal band
    Fought bravely to defend their flag,
How could they see the Stars and Stripes
    Supplanted by the rebel rag!

All honor to the noble few
    Who held the fort so long and well!
To them the victor's crown is due
    Unconquered, though their fortress fell.

"Fort Sumter's taken!" At the word
    The people rose with sudden start,
All party feuds were laid aside,
    Hand joined with hand and heart with heart.

And when the summons issued forth
  From Washington for arms and men,
It found the people of the North
  Prepared to meet the summons then.

The old Bay State, with eager zeal
  As ever, foremost for the right,
Sent forth her armies to the field
  For freedom and for truth to fight.

What other State upon its page
  Such record as our own can show
Of Statesmen true, of soldiers brave
  To Union pledged, come weal, come woe?

The noble men of long ago
  Are treasured in our memory yet;
What soldiers who have faced the foe
  Sumner or Andrew can forget?

The fountain that poured forth its flood
  At Lexington in days of yore,
Is still as pure, and gave its blood
  To cleanse the streets of Baltimore.

Our own fair town of Pilgrim stock
  Was not a whit behind the rest;
Unflinching as her Plymouth Rock,
  She gave her bravest and her best.

From every rank, from every lot
  Her men were marshalled for the strife;
From mansion proud, from humble cot,
  They came to save the nation's life.

They left their homes, a noble band
  In health and youthful vigor strong,
To save from death their native land,
  Maintain the right, put down the wrong.

Though firm and fearless, who can tell
  The anguish of the parting hour?
When called to say the last farewell
  To meet, perchance, on earth no more.

Then rose to Heaven the earnest prayer
   That God their loved ones would defend,
Would guard them with his tender care,
   And keep them safely to the end.

Then came the real " tug of war."
   The daily drill in fort and camp,
The toilsome march to scenes afar,
   The sentry's lonely midnight tramp.

The battlefield, the scanty fare,
   The dreadful work of shot and shell,
The sickening swamp, the tainted air,
   The nurse's ward, the prison cell.

Not those alone who risked their lives
   In mountain gorge or Southern plain,
But mothers, sisters, daughters, wives
   Had their full share of grief and pain.

The waiting for the Daily News,
   To read of battles lost or won,
Dreading its columns to peruse
   Lest they report some loved one gone.

What sorrows brings the message brief !
   The awful waste of human life ;
The gentle maiden's untold grief,
   The childless home, the widowed wife.

The God of battles was their trust,
   What need had they to be afraid ?
God on their side, their cause was just,
   On him their fainting hearts were stayed.

He heard in Heaven the bitter cries
   Of those in bonds—He saw their pain ;
There needed some great sacrifice
   To purge the nation from its stain.

The victory's won ! The war is o'er !
   All honor to the soldiers brave !
United States we stand once more,
   Land of the free, without a slave.

Four million slaves, as cattle driven,
   Now walk erect as freemen bold,
Their chains are broke, their bonds are riven,
   No more can they be bought or sold.

The Flag that for a hundred years
   Has been an emblem of the free
Now floats again o'er every State
   O'er North and South, from sea to sea.

But where are those, so stout of heart,
   Who left us when the war begun?
Those who so nobly bore their part
   Where are they now the victory's won?

Go, read the Records of your town!
   What's written 'gainst each soldier's name,
Of suffering borne, of actions done,
   Should place it on the roll of fame.

The mournful Record says of *one*,
   "At Sabine Cross Roads he was killed,"
Of *others*, "Died at Baton Rouge."
   For them with grief our hearts are filled.

Cane River, Richmond, Antietam
   The Wilderness and New Orleans,
The Hospital, the Prison van
   And Petersburg saw parting scenes.

Point Lookout, Alexandria
   And Morgan's Bend sad tales can tell
Of those our friends and comrades true
   Who in the cause of Freedom fell.

And some upon the ocean wave
   The Record says, laid down their lives,
The seaman as the soldier brave
   Offered a willing sacrifice.

The rebel gunboat Merrimac
   Found men who by their flag would stand,
When by its murderous attack,
   The Congress sunk, and Cumberland.

Full well that father knew his son
  As he in pride and sorrow said,
When told the flag was taken down,
  "It must be, then, that Joe is dead."*

Such was the stuff that made our men
  Invincible on land and sea,
That made our country what it is,
  "Land of the Brave, Home of the Free."

A debt of gratitude we owe
  To those who died that we might live;
How can we our affection show?
  What tribute to their memory give?

By us they'll never be forgot,
  But *we* shall soon have passed away,
Others will rise who knew them not;
  Then let us our sad tribute pay.

To them a MONUMENT we'll raise
  That shall endure when we are gone
To tell their deeds in notes of praise
  To generations yet unborn.

The "Boston Monument" will stand
  An honor to the city's heart,
The glow of pride that filled the land
  Will never from our breasts depart.

We would in our more humble way
  The example follow Boston set,
And raise a monument to say
  Our Heroes we will ne'er forget.

---

* The fullest and most authentic account of the destruction of the "Congress," which I have seen, is that by Frederick H. Curtis, who was a Hanover boy and a gunner of that vessel. This account is given by another Hanover citizen, Frank S. Alger, in the New England Magazine for February, 1899. I scarcely need say that the father of Joseph B. Smith, the Captain of the Congress, was Admiral Joseph Smith who was a native of Hanover.

Consult the Record book once more;
  What says it of the remnant left?
"Disabled, wounded, sick and sore,
  Of health and all its joys bereft."

For blessings which we dearly prize
  Our soldiers we can ne'er repay,
But let us do what in us lies
  To prove our love without delay.

Oh, let us rear within our State
  A home for those who need our care,
Amid our own beloved scenes,
  Our hills and vales, our native air.

The homesick soldier needs to rest
  Where he can meet the friends he loves,
May he with such a home be blest
  And never more be forced to rove.

And now the Olive Branch of peace
  Waves o'er our land from shore to shore.
May strife and all contention cease,
  And wars and fightings be no more.

The *patriot spirit* has not fled,
  We love our country and her laws,
In memory of our honored dead
  We pledge ourselves to freedom's cause.

May Justice, Temperance, Truth and Love
  O'er all our land have perfect sway,
May He who rules in Heaven above
  Lead every heart in wisdom's way.

Then shall the land that gave us birth
  By righteousness exalted be
Among the nations of the earth—
  "Land of the Brave, Home of the Free."

Conclusion.

It is with feelings of sadness that we have to say the Hanover Academy is now permanently closed. The property is indeed leased to the town for school purposes, and we trust it will be so used in the future, but it will never be Hanover Academy. The founders of this Academy and those who contributed towards the erection of our beautiful building never expected or dreamed of such a result as this. Let us listen again to some words from the dedication address of Rev. Mr. Dyer. " Your work," he says, " contemplates blessing not one neighborhood only, but many. The structure you have reared is substantial. You expect the feet of more than one generation of youths will cross its threshold to obtain instruction within its consecrated walls. And doubtless, long after most of you who have been deeply interested and actively engaged in its erection shall have been gathered to your fathers, this noble edifice, standing where you have reared it, and proffering the advantages of an Academic education to all, will welcome to its halls a multitude of those who shall come after you on the journey of life. Your children's children will eat the fruit of the tree you have planted, and sit down under its shadow with great delight. And this institution, so cherished by you who have furnished to learning this beautiful asylum, will exert on this community its enlightening, elevating, refining influences, possibly till *they* themselves shall cease to be any longer interested in all that is done under the sun. . . . As friends of Education and lovers of our race, we cannot help casting our eye down the long vista of the future to contemplate the blessings which will flow from this humble seat of learning to generations yet unborn."

But it may be asked if the blessings thus contemplated and hoped for will not be secured if this property shall forever be devoted, as we hope it may be, to public school uses.* Doubtless this would be so in part, but no public school in its influence can exactly fill the place of an Academy. For a student to leave the public school for a private school of a high grade where he or his parents or guardians would have to pay money, is a much more important step than to leave one common school for another, even though the latter be of a higher grade. Such a step has been to many even in our community a turning point for life, inasmuch as it supposes or will naturally beget a purpose and determination to study by putting forth some special effort and at some personal cost. And then the personnel of such private school and the *esprit de corps* of such school companionship are naturally of a higher kind, and are different in quality and degree from what our public schools commonly or naturally yield. Such private schools and academies, pervaded as generally in the past with a Christian spirit and influence, have thus done a great and blessed work in the world. Professor Cecil F. P. Bancroft, who has just finished a quarter centennial as Principal of Phillips Andover Academy, says: "The

---

* We understand that the Salmond heirs, who own nearly half the Academic property are willing, in order that the same be not wholly diverted from its original school purposes, to donate their share to the town for a permanant public school. It is also thought that several other stockholders are willing to dispose of their part of the property in a similar manner. Should this plan be carried out, I should favor the suggestion which has been made that this should be called the "Salmond School." We should then have two schools in town, this and the new "Curtis School" on Main St., which would be worthily named.

Academies are now doing for the whole country, especially for territory not reached by the public high school, and for individuals in all parts of the land, a work which no other agency has been found to do equally well. An Academy, protected from political, parental and local interference, does its work for boys and girls separated to a studious life, with a singleness of responsibility for the entire time and the entire nurture of the pupils which a public school cannot and ought not to assume, and develops an independence of character which is the best preparation for a successful career. Most of the Academies were planted under religious motives and the note of Christian character is dominant."

But times have changed. "High schools" are now established in almost every town, and Normal schools in many of our counties, and thus private schools and academies, unless amply funded, must naturally suffer and decline and cease to be. An Academy can now live and flourish only as it has an endowment well nigh equal to that of an ordinary college. We have a few, and only a few, of such secondary schools at present in our Commonwealth, while most of our old and even once flourishing academies are now things of the past. But these academies did not all die easily; at least Hanover Academy did not. Since my connection with it in its decline and decease, I have found that its branches overshadowed the land, and that its roots extended to the remotest States of the Union. Again and again, yea, often have I been surprised at receiving letters from the most distant States asking for information, circulars and catalogues. With a comparatively slight endowment, such as I have repeatedly sought to gain.

Hanover Academy, with its amazing vitality, might be in a flourishing condition not only to this day but for many years to come. I should be glad to think that this Academy might possibly be revived. Some Academies are being thus reopened, like that at Milton, which has just celebrated its centennial. It was closed in 1866 when the Milton High School was established, but in 1884 it was reopened and now has a list of 135 pupils. And President Eliot of Harvard University said at this celebration that " this revival of academies has gone on in many other parts of New England, and that the academy was never so strong in our country as it is to-day." But as I have said, most of our academies are things of the past, and will not appear again, though their influence will never cease to be. Let us be thankful for their past existence, and for the great and good work which they accomplished in their generation. Let us also be thankful that our humble HANOVER ACADEMY has no slight share in this great and good work accomplished.

William P. Duncan, Esq., "a former pupil," under date of Cambridge, Sept. 1, 1898, sends us the following lines on

THE PASSING OF HANOVER ACADEMY.

> When we were young, when we were young,
> Impatient of the years,
> We did not care in youth so fair,
> To trace life's hopes and fears.
> Now we are old, now we are old,
> Our memory scans the past,
> And days of yore, we live them o'er,
> Too beautiful to last.

HISTORY OF HANOVER ACADEMY.

The classic school in grove so cool,
  In rural town of old,
In thought we greet, again we meet
  Our playmates gay and bold.
How doth it seem but as a dream
  Or "weavers' shuttle" swift,
The passing on of time agone
  As lightning through the rift.

Now we are old, now we are old,
  The school has ceased to be.
Our hearts will burn, oft as we turn
  In retrospection free.
Yet now farewell! We break the spell
  Of memory fond and true;
Sweet classic shades! our vision fades,
  We sadly say adieu.

www.ingramcontent.com/pod-product-compliance
Lightning Source LLC
Chambersburg PA
CBHW031813230426
43669CB00009B/1127